DANCING
WITH YOUR
DARK HORSE

[About the Author]

Surprisingly, internationally renowned equestrian coach, widely-read columnist, and author of *Horses Don't Lie* Chris Irwin did not grow up with horses. It wasn't until after high school while searching for a career that offered a sense of purpose in life that his quest led him to Longacres Racetrack in Seattle. At the track, immersed in life with the thoroughbred horses, Chris found his calling. His passion for exploring horsemanship then drew him to training and driving draft horse teams, where he went on to win many competitions, including the Calgary Stampede. Soon he was training champions in combined driving. By his early thirties, Chris achieved eighteen U.S. National Championships in both riding and driving events with Nevada's wild Mustangs. As he became known as the trainer who could turn around the most challenging "problem horses," Chris was called into the higher levels of dressage and jumping.

Chris' methods, considered to be the "evolution within the natural horsemanship revolution," have been highlighted on television shows such as *Canada AM*, *The Discovery Channel*, *Mustang: America's Wild Horse*, and the PBS show *Horse N' Around*. He has produced an acclaimed instructional video series and plays a leading educational role at The Secretariat Center for thoroughbred retraining in Lexington, Kentucky and with the U.S. government-sponsored Wild Mustang Adoption Program. His highly successful Train the Trainer program operates from six North American locations.

Chris lives with his wife Kathryn in northwest Alberta, Canada, where they will begin development of their Riversong Ranch Equestrian Retreat in spring of 2005.

Bob Weber is a journalist and author based in Edmonton, Alberta, Canada.

CHRIS IRWIN

WITH BOB WEBER

DANCING
WITH YOUR
DARK HORSE

How Horse Sense Helps Us Find

Balance, Strength and Wisdom

MARLOWE & COMPANY
NEW YORK

DANCING WITH YOUR DARK HORSE:
How Horse Sense Helps Us Find Balance, Strength and Wisdom

Copyright © 2005 by Chris Irwin

Published by
Marlowe & Company
An Imprint of Avalon Publishing Group Incorporated
245 West 17th Street • 11th floor
New York, NY 10011

AVALON
publishing group incorporated

Library of Congress Cataloging-in-Publication Data
Irwin, Chris.
Dancing with your dark horse : how horse sense helps us find balance,
strength, and wisdom / Chris Irwin with Bob Weber.
p. cm.
ISBN 1-56924-387-5 (pbk.)
1. Horses—Behavior. 2. Horses—Training. 3. Human-animal communication.
I. Weber, Bob. II. Title.
SF281.I78 2005
636.1'0835—dc22
2005005845

9 8 7 6 5 4 3 2

DESIGNED BY PAULINE NEUWIRTH, NEUWIRTH AND ASSOCIATES, INC.

Printed in the United States of America

For Raven and Adler
Spread your wings my little ones
Dare to dream
Believe
and fly

"When He broke the third seal, I heard the third living creature saying, 'Come!' I looked, and behold, a black horse; and he who sat on it had a pair of scales in his hand."

REVELATION 6:5

[Contents]

DANCING
WITH YOUR
DARK HORSE

[1]

off my high horse

ORSE WHISPERERS CAN'T walk on water. While it is true that some of us teachers and trainers in the horse world strive to walk the spiritual path of a modern-day shaman, there are those who choose to embrace the limelight of a traveling showman. A long time ago, I chose the shaman's way of the road-less-traveled. Or maybe it chose me. Either way, I felt a calling to give back to the world what I had received from the horses because back when I had every reason to give up on the human race for good, it was the horses that rescued my soul and renewed my passion for living. I've spent so many years living and working with them that at times I still feel I understand horses better than humans. From the moment I first walked into a barn, I related to the anger the horses expressed with their twirling heads and wringing tails, the confusion and sullenness of their low-headed stares, the fears so painfully obvious in their tightly clamped tails, the frustration of their pawing, their bites of resentment, even the playful exultation of their powerful thundering across a wide-open meadow. I learned how to read and listen to the body language of horses to such a degree that I fully understood where they were coming from, and I vowed to be their voice.

But as I look back on the past twenty-five years of my career, especially the recent events that rocked the very foundation of my being, I see now that my approach may have more often resembled a "Sermon on the Mount"—bittersweetly sugar-coated with righteous indignation, condemnation, even condescension. They say that pride precedes the fall. What I realize now is that, in my desire to "fight the good fight," I did indeed get up on my high horse and set myself up for a terrible fall.

If what happened to me the day my shadow self reared its ugly head happened to me now, I'd say "bring it on" and I'd know how to deal with it. In fact, I'd welcome it. I've traveled a long and painfully difficult path since that pivotal horsemanship clinic just over a year ago, a path that is, in large part, the subject of this book. But back then my reaction was fear, confusion, and despair. It was the natural result, I suppose, of kidding myself that I had it all figured out. I was on top of my little world and as far as I was concerned it was only going to get bigger. Boy, was I wrong. When I look back at it now, my comeuppance seems inevitable, just as paddling upstream on a placid prairie river inevitably leads back to turbulent mountain headwaters. But the wisdom of hindsight wasn't available to me then, and what came at me that day seemed to come out of nowhere. It was as if a sunny sky suddenly darkened and out of roiling thunderclouds a horse appeared, a dark chestnut, bloodred, barely discernible amidst the shadows but bearing down on me hard.

The morning started out, however, as just another day at the office. In my case, that's not a cubicle with a computer but a round pen in a riding arena alongside a grandstand. I've seen thousands of such pens by now, from those at international equestrian events to private stables tucked away in the hills, and they're a lot alike. The same earthy smell, the same ascending benches filled with expectant faces, the same scuffed-up rails encircling the space where it all takes place. This is my domain and I strode into it like a maestro ascending the podium. It was my forty-third birthday, and I was marking it by doing what I did best, fully expecting it to be yet another successful event.

After all, I'd had hundreds of similar days. As a successful horse trainer/gentler/whisperer (insert your own favorite buzzword here), I seem to spend most of my life giving demonstrations and clinics in round pens like this. I work with some of the best, most challenging, and most demanding people and horses in the equestrian world. I've given hundreds of workshops (which we call clinics in the horse biz) all over North America and beyond. I run my own certification programs in the United States and Canada where I train other trainers in the methods I've developed. After numerous translations and printings there are now so many copies of my previous book circulating around the world that I still hear from people who have been touched by *Horses Don't Lie* six years after it was first published. Nor have my readers and students been limited to horse enthusiasts. I'm proud to say people from all walks of life have drawn inspiration from the lessons horses have taught me. I've given experiential workshops on communication and leadership skills with horses to teachers, lawyers, mental health professionals, corporate executives, entrepreneurs, and I've found myself exchanging ideas with captains of industry. My columns are very well received in some of the horse world's most influential magazines—even when I'm bucking trends in the horse world.

In fact, I'd just published a little article that had added to my notoriety. I wrote that I was growing increasingly frustrated and even angry over some directions I was seeing people going with horses. Showmanship and flimflam were slowly strangling the movement to which I'd dedicated my life, I wrote. Too many "horse whisperers" or "natural horsemen," and also a few gurus within the emerging phenomenon of horses used in self-help workshops and psychotherapy, were preying on an easy-to-impress public. The round pen, something I had come to regard as a sacred space of open doors and magical possibilities, was degenerating into a circus ring. Facile trickery was replacing the true understanding that can often result in meaningful change for both human and horse. Fake shamans who should have known better were throwing people at horses without giving them any real insight into what they were doing. The results were predictable. Well-meaning, horse-loving people whose only crime was lack of knowledge were being short-changed and innocent horses were being confused, and inadvertently abused. "Used" as props to sell "signature lines" of tack like the latest halter or lead rope, along with books, videos, and T-shirts. The stableside controversy generated by my little article and the Internet buzz it created in the chat rooms frequented by horse folk was both substantial and welcome—because I believed in my message and also because I was gratified and a little flattered that I was able to sway people with my words.

I don't want to spell out my entire résumé here, but I'm trying to make a point. After years of hard work and a long string of successes, I had achieved a position of significant leadership in the horse industry and, in some circles, beyond. People count on me to show them it's possible to quiet and calm a frightened or angry horse without violence. Instead of forcing or coercing a horse into becoming a beast of burden, my students learn how to think like a horse and how to play horse games by horse rules. Horse training becomes horseplay as we compete with horses to earn their respect, focus, trust, and willingness by having the right stuff to be seen by them as "the better horse."

It may seem like a huge leap, but, most often, my students take the next step—applying those horse sense principles to other areas of their life—by and for themselves. But they learn them through me. I am a teacher; and teachers are, or I believe they should be, leaders.

So it was with that mingled sense of accomplishment, pride, and responsibility behind me that I walked into the equestrian center that day. To be honest, I was drawing heavily on that blend of character to get me through. For one thing, I was tired down to my boots. I'm on the road over two hundred days a year so I'm more than used to a life of traveling, but that morning I was feeling the toll my marathon work schedule was taking on me. I was just plain worn out. I felt I wasn't quite all there, as if I'd left little pieces of my heart and soul behind in all the round pens I'd seen over the last few months and they hadn't quite caught back up with me yet. Like an old war-horse, I felt I'd been ridden hard and put away wet.

I had another reason for wanting to be somewhere else. I'd been coming to this stable for a few years and I had some history here. I'd agreed to do a short demonstration when I thought I was going to be in the area anyway to speak at a convention over the weekend. However, at the last minute, the convention was postponed, and instead of canceling the demonstration, I somehow wound up agreeing to add to it with a full weekend of private lessons at this boarding and training stable owned by one of my students. My heart wasn't in it, and yet for practical and financial reasons, there I was. That was my first mistake.

Still, people had gathered and were expecting something. Suck it up, I told myself. I knew I couldn't disappoint them, and I didn't think I would, either. I'd done a thousand demonstrations like this, tired and out of sorts or not. I hitched up my onstage attitude and ambled over to my office, the round pen.

The gig that day was to be a demonstration of herd dynamics. I was performing for a full house and the grandstands were full of people keen to watch me work and listen to me talk about how horses relate to each other in a natural setting and how leadership and the herd hierarchy is established and used. It's a fascinating subject and one that I always look forward to speaking on. I sized up the crowd. There were plenty of families with children on hand for the day but I knew it would be a pretty sophisticated group, full of people familiar with the horse whisperer shtick and perfectly able to figure out for themselves what's really going on between a man and a horse. I say this because I recognized that many if not most of them had been to my clinics in the past. I greeted everyone and signaled for the horses to be brought in. "Let the games begin," I said.

And right away, I knew something was wrong.

In preparation, I'd asked for three horses who were used to living with each other and who were regularly turned out to pasture together. That way, they would have already worked out for themselves the pecking order among them. I'd be able to point out the body language gestures they communicate with, interpret how it affected their behavior together and explain how to work with herd dynamics in a language they understood to develop authority and the position of leadership in a way that's seen as somewhat more natural to the horse. But the three horses that were brought in met my request in no way at all. I began to clue in when they were brought in separately. And very quickly, it became crystal clear: I was looking not at three herd buddies but at three alpha mares who were not at all pleased to be in each other's company. (I learned later that the three were, in fact, never turned out together because their owners thought they'd hurt each other.) I began my spiel, but I didn't get very far. Those "bad to the bone" girls got right into it, kicking, striking, biting, and going at each other with a vengeance. Things quickly degenerated into a very ugly kickfest, with two of the mares ganging up on the third. I had no choice but to jump into the round pen to try to separate them before they seriously injured each other.

It was like being in a back alley brawl with an entire gang. Aside from the extreme violence, the mares were doing the horse equivalent of shouting threats and insults at each other so loudly the noise and adrenaline had driven every other thought out of their brains. The only thing I could do was to simulate the horses' language of bold gestures and dramatic movements and shout even louder, distracting them and focusing their attention on me. I cracked the lunge whip loud and hard into the air and pushed them and pushed them (I'll explain what I mean in a later chapter) until I got their attention. I began to herd them and get them moving the way a horse would, reasoning that it would be better to keep them busy "on the go" rather than have them stop and start attacking each other again. Before too long I had all three mares thundering inside the perimeter of the

CEALY TETLEY

It took three men using chains around his nose to lead this aggressive pinto warmblood stallion into the arena at the Captial Classic, a grand prix jumping show in Ottawa, where Chris was giving demonstrations on "being the better horse." Note that Chris is wearing a microphone and while he is "dancing" with the stallion he is giving a detailed play-by-play interpretation of his techniques to an audience of 5000 onlookers

LAURA SIMPSON

Only twenty minutes later Chris and the stallion have bonded and are able to walk around the show grounds with no problem at all.

round pen, freshly harrowed earth flying up from under their hooves into the slanting light. I separated the two that had been doing the ganging-up and rushed them out of the gate to the waiting grooms, who were staring at me as if in shock.

Shock was also written all over the third horse, quivering at the far side of the round pen. Stella stood stiff-legged, her head high and rigid. Her eyes were wide, staring, and fixed. A bloodred chestnut mare, big, more than sixteen hands high, with every nerve lit up and humming like a bug zapper. She looked back at me and I'm sure she saw the same thing staring back at her. It's no joke jumping into the middle of all that whirling, blind-mad horseflesh, and I, too, was dizzy with relief and adrenaline. If I'd paused for a breath or two, I would have realized that I was also in shock. And one of the first things to go when you're in shock is judgment. Proof: I decided I would work with this horse.

Partly, I just wanted to get close to the chestnut and ask her to trot a few steps so that I could see if she still moved soundly. I was concerned that the other two horses had hurt her in the scrap. But I was also feeling a little twinge of offended professional pride. I was beginning to suspect I'd been set up, something that happens sometimes to people in my line of work. I had the feeling that the barn manager (who had a history of testing my boundaries) had decided it would be cute to throw the big-time horse guy a little equine curve ball and see if he could hit it. Part of me was probably thinking, "Okay, I'll show you I'm not so easily rattled." I was also feeling the spur of my position. A leader can't disappoint, I felt, and I had to give the crowd "something." Looking back, that's how I probably rationalized it at the time, but in truth, I now realize that I was just fired up and angry at being toyed with. People had seen me off balance. Even though it was just for a moment, I didn't like that. My first mistake now led to my second mistake. Instead of being concerned about what was good for the horse, I was suddenly more concerned about what was good for Chris Irwin, so-called horseman extraordinaire.

Outwardly, I kept my professional cool. I didn't get where I am by letting audiences down, and I stepped forward. "Ladies and gentlemen," I said. "I can't do a demonstration of herd dynamics with these three horses. There's no way these three ever naturally would be or could be so close together in such a confined space. So, if you don't mind, there'll be a slight change in program. We just saw an example of how horses sometimes 'play'—and yes, it can get extremely primal at times. Now let's tone the game down a little while I demonstrate and explain how to play a different kind of horse game, still by horse rules, to establish yourself as a leader, with just this one horse."

I took up my lunge whip, the grooms opened the round-pen gate, and I walked into the round pen with Stella. I began as I always do. I took up my position, slightly back of her girth, telling her to "go," a message I underlined with a gentle little flick of the whip from a low underhand swing into the air in the direction of her flanks. And, as is natural and relaxing to a horse, she started to do just that, trotting around the perimeter of the ring. She was still tense and angry for sure, but Stella was moving. This was what I had expected. This was what almost always happens. Showing a horse that you're there to motivate its movement is the opposite message of trying to catch or capture it. It's the first step in getting a horse to trust you, and I probably started to allow myself to exhale. What came next, however, was something that had never happened to me before, something that shook my confidence to the core.

As Stella trotted around the pen, I backed up a little, easing off on the herding push while I repositioned myself so that I would come up in front of her as she came around the circular pen. Horses avoid allowing anything into the space around their faces, and my intent was to use this to block her current direction and then turn her in to the center of the circle, sending her off the opposite way. Causing her to turn would reinforce the dominant position I was starting to establish with regard to who pushes whom. Stella, however, had other ideas.

Before I realized what was happening, Stella bolted toward me and knocked me aside with her shoulder like a bruising fullback playing for keeps at the Super Bowl. It was disturbing, but I'd dealt with plenty of overly aggressive horses before. While keeping up a line of self-deprecating patter to the audience, I stepped to the center of the ring and held out my hand aimed toward Stella's face to block her as she ran past. I was like a traffic cop indicating that the road into my space was closed. I swear she snarled as she ran into me again. And this time, she didn't stop. She began plowing around me in tight little circles, bunting into me with her left shoulder, like an enraged bull getting the better of a stunned matador. She had completely taken control of the round pen. Instead of me herding her, she was bullying me! As I stumbled and struggled to keep my balance in the soft footing, I could see from the glazed look in her eyes that Stella wasn't reacting to me. She was still responding to those two mares who had tried to maim her. She thought she was fighting for her life. And I could see from the cue of her head flipping higher and higher straight up into the air that she was threatening me with rearing up. It's intimidating enough when a horse rears up on you from ten feet back, but Stella was right on top of me and her only way down would have been right through my thick skull. All of a sudden, just when I thought I had oiled the troubled waters and that everything was going to be all roses and olive branches, I was in serious trouble. And not just for my professional reputation, but also for my safety. Stella kept coming at me relentlessly and for the very first time in my long professional career; I got the hell out of that round pen!

I managed a little more patter for the crowd. "With horses we need to be able to read them well enough to know when to advance, when to stand our ground, and when to retreat. And once in a blue moon…," I said, grinning feebly, "when to run."

But inwardly, I was struggling to maintain control—and not doing too well. Clearly, someone had let this horse develop some extremely dangerous habits. (I found out later she'd also chased the barn manager out of the pen and had routinely dragged her owner up and down the barn aisle like a rag doll on a rope.) I told myself that, surely, I had a duty to correct those habits before Stella hurt somebody. I couldn't let her develop a taste for intimidating people. Giving up would be the wrong message for both Stella and the audience. Then there was my own liability—hadn't a horse trainer in British Columbia recently been killed because of her failure to handle a stallion that kicked her in the head? But while those concerns were sincere, something else was going on inside me that I was less willing to acknowledge. For the first time in my life, a horse had pushed me backward. For the first time, I didn't stand my ground. For the first time, a horse forced me out of the round pen. I couldn't believe what I had just allowed to happen. I had never walked away from a horse in the round pen. Wounded pride had combined with the anger I felt at being "pushed around," and the combination was toxic. My second mistake was about to lead to my third.

It wouldn't have been easy, but I could have switched tactics and put a halter on her and done some in-hand work with her, getting her to lower her head. In horses, this releases natural endorphins, and the relaxed, feel-good effect of endorphins is what this horse needed more than anything. However, I was being a "purist," determined to deal with Stella "animal to animal," with no strings attached, just like a dominant horse would go about showing her who is boss. I was no longer thinking about feel-good anything. From outside the pen, I stepped up on the bottom rail of the fence around the pen and cracked the whip loudly into the air, trying to push Stella off again. She charged toward the fence, slamming into it so hard the whole thing shook and rattled. The audience gasped! Her aggression toward me only made me more determined to impose my will and I kept at it until I eventually got her charging around the pen, her head high and her nostrils flaring in rage. Three times, I thought I had her where I wanted her and tried to climb back into the pen. Three times, she chased me out.

Finally, on my fourth attempt, forty-five minutes after I began, Stella was ready to allow me to stay in the ring with her. I wasn't making little jokes with the audience anymore. I was hardly even aware of the people in the grandstand, who were staring in shocked silence. For a moment, Stella and I glared at each other. Then we began to see who would end up herding whom. For three hours we kept at it. It's hard to describe what happened other than to say it was primal combat. Stella stormed around the pen. I dodged her lunges. Whenever she got too close I defended myself with the short, stiff dressage whip I'd brought in with me as I tried to push her off of me and into the direction I wanted her to go. I wasn't trying to gentle Stella or teach her anything about trust. I was simply trying to subdue her—and, just as enraged, she was refusing to submit. It was a battle of wills, with both of us too stubborn, defiant, and unwilling to give in. When the dust finally cleared, Stella was peppered with welts, nasty little bruises from the dressage whip. And I wasn't much better. The next morning, I couldn't walk, and I was stiff and painfully sore for days. There had been no "join-up," no communing of man and beast. Stella and I had stared at each other from opposite sides of the pen, both too tired to fight any more yet too stoic to admit defeat. At best, it was a truce. If I'd felt tired at the start of the demonstration, I now felt as shattered as a bombed-out house. I stood, lost in an altered state of surreal exhaustion, as a groom led Stella away.

Then I remembered the audience and I looked up to the grandstand. Most of the onlookers—and all of the families—had left. The few that were left stared back at me, appalled. They had come for an entertaining and informative afternoon of Disney and I'd suddenly switched channels over to the crueler forces of nature often found on the more graphic, reality-based wilderness shows found on networks like the Discovery Channel. They had, they thought, just seen me do everything I had preached against for so long. I'd beaten on a horse and abused it. And worst of all, I felt as if they might be right. I thought back to the fine words I'd penned in that recent column I was so proud of. Who was using and abusing the horse for his own purposes now?

The next few days were among the blackest I've had since I entered this business. Everybody at the stable still showed up for the private lessons they'd signed up for, but our conversations were stilted, as if we were talking about everything except what we needed to. I could sense that people were wondering about the famous horse whisperer. Over the next week I got a few letters and e-mails all but calling me a hypocrite and a fraud. I also had supporters, people who told me that Stella had needed the correcting I'd given her, but they weren't able to silence the doubt pounding like hoofbeats inside me. I went back through the chain of events and picked out where I thought I had made mistakes, but that didn't seem to explain how things had gotten so terribly out of hand. Nor did those mistakes seem to explain the powerful anger, disgust, and confusion I was feeling inside myself.

When I look back at it now, the thoughts and feelings that tortured me are hard to describe. I'd been working with horses for nearly twenty-five years. At first, I did it just because it felt good. In a way I didn't yet understand, it was a healing balm for hurts deep inside me and I followed that healing instinctively. But over the years, it grew to be something much more. Horses became a spiritual as well as a professional path and I had followed my quest with all my heart. The daily routines of horsemanship became rituals for me, and those rituals had brought me so close to the world of nature that I became tuned in to every breeze, each cry of the coyote, and every call of the raven. I soaked it all up and reflected on the meaning of every encounter I had. I felt that horses were leading me closer and closer to something infinite and eternal. And I never doubted my progress along that path. The horses were my medicine. And I, in turn, was their champion. But now I somehow felt betrayed by them and also by myself. Something had erupted inside me and turned everything inside out. I felt I had let down everyone I had ever known. I felt naked and exposed. I felt I had done something so monstrous that it was a dead certainty that the industry that had lauded me so highly was now going to turn on me. I had committed a highly public act of self-sabotage. I had been tried and found guilty. I was a surfer losing control while riding the one big wave I'd waited for all my life and now there was nothing left but to be flung about and battered in the foam and tossed up on the beach. And what was I going to do? Horses were all I knew.

I swear, I felt so bad that I considered chucking the whole thing and just going back to quietly training easy horses on a ranch somewhere. My newlywed wife, Kathryn, who had given up her own successful career managing resort hotels to join me in mine, had never seen me like this. Kathryn wasn't there that night. But she knew in my voice over the phone that something horrible had happened. And while she deserves a lot of credit for helping build and manage our business, one of the greatest contributions she'll ever make was the acceptance and understanding she gave me during those weeks and months of hell. She kept me going.

I still had no answers a few days later in Toronto, where I had my next appearance. I hadn't felt so apprehensive about walking out in front of an audience since I started out. I feared I could no longer trust myself to listen to the horse and respond appropriately with what it needed to hear. And wouldn't you know, the first horse to be worked with was a big, black, dramatic Friesian stallion, full of energy and aggression. I ran through a silent prayer and set to work, relying on my years of experience with these magnificent animals to get me through. Thank God, within minutes he came around, joining up with me in that openhearted, generous way that horses have. I was relieved and grateful. It was going to be okay, I thought.

But Stella wasn't through with me yet. That afternoon with the bloodred mare wouldn't let me go. It tightened around my thoughts like a cinch. Although this was by far the most intense conflict I had ever been involved in with a horse, I'd had unpleasant experiences with horses before. And God knows, everyone who's spent any time near a barn has seen things go south. But what was it about this one that made me feel so bad? Why was I haunted by such guilt?

Over the following weeks and months, as I traveled around the continent, I puzzled over what my episode with Stella was doing to me. As I thought and meditated, something began to stir within me, something I'd managed to repress up until now. I began to sense that something was dangerously out of balance inside me. Something that felt familiar, as if it had been growing in me a long time, maybe all my life. It had been quiet for some time now, and I had almost forgotten it existed. But Stella had stirred it up. Deep in my heart, the hoofbeats of a dark horse were beginning to drum an echo to hers. It was a long time before I finally understood what was happening inside me. Meanwhile, guilt was eating away at me, making me fester with anger, frustration, and disillusionment. The emotions were confusing and painful. I was surprised at how much hurt some of that old poison could still cause. But Stella had done me a life-saving favor. She had shown me the door to my healing—deep and dark though it seemed. And once I understood her message, I realized that every horse I'd ever worked with had been trying to teach me the same lesson all along. I just hadn't been ready, willing, or able to hear their message.

a horse of a different color

*B*ACK WHEN I was just starting out, I struck up a bit of a friendship with an old farrier who worked the same stables I did. A lifetime of being around horses in close quarters, tending to their hooves and fitting them with new shoes, had taught him a thing or two and I had the good luck to be on the receiving end of some of his wisdom. "A horse has to go forward even to back up" was one of his sayings, and it's true. Movement to a horse is like shelter to a human. It's where they live, a basic and fundamental necessity of life. Horses solve all their problems, from finding food to fleeing danger to establishing who's going to be boss in the herd, with this one simple strategy. Birds fly, fish swim, and horses keep moving. Nothing comes more naturally to a horse than forward movement. Stories, however, don't always work like that. Before I can go forward with this one, I have to back up a little.

My first book, *Horses Don't Lie,* told the story of how I tapped into an old understanding of horses and horsemanship, an understanding based in the knowledge of how horses understand and interact with their world and how that differs from the human approach. Eventually, I came to realize that working with horses in this way not only gave me a powerful and profound partnership with horses, it also changed the way I viewed everything around me. Connecting with horses on this level changed my life. And since then, it's changed the lives of hundreds, even thousands, of others. These basic concepts underpin this book as well, and at the risk of repeating myself to previous readers, I need to discuss them for a while.

I didn't grow up with horses—which may have been just as well, for I didn't have inherited equine assumptions to unlearn when I started to figure out things for myself, a process I began in my teens shortly after I quit school and ran away from home. Neither place had been remotely close to happy for me, and for a while, I was just glad to be away. For a few years, I combined winter ski-bumming at various resorts in the Canadian Rockies with grunt work at several racing and riding stables in the summer. Slowly, by the early '80s, I drifted south into Nevada, mucking out stalls and feeding and caring for horses, and I was learning a few things about being around them. It was just basic stuff, like staying out of a horse's face. Or like how personal space is a really big deal to them. Or how if you make them mad or annoy them, they often turn their butt to you. In all, the most important lesson was that each horse has its own unique personality. The old saying is true—a horse has a mind of its own.

I was more or less stumbling along, spending a lot of time on horseback and learning as I went. Eventually, I got a job "starting" horses, which basically meant getting them used to the idea of allowing themselves to be ridden while taking orders from a human. I had a vague idea of being as gentle on them as I could, but looking back I'd have to say it was still pretty rough—until I had a major riding accident when a friend and I were galloping full tilt through some pretty rugged country in the mountains above Lake Tahoe. I did a lot of that in those days and I suppose I was a little overconfident. A thoroughbred by the name of Rocky and I were putting some distance on my buddy and his horse and I turned around to give him a little friendly ragging. At that moment, my horse stumbled in a soft spot and we went down, flipping over the edge of the trail and tumbling on down the side of the mountain. Through the rocks, sage, and manzanita we fell together, battered and torn, until we finally came to a stop with me crushed and pinned underneath Rocky. I was still partially in the saddle. It took that old racehorse three desperate swings of his entire body before he could get his legs up and under him to stand up on the side of the steep slope. And with each thrashing attempt I felt the saddle horn bludgeon my chest and break another rib. When Rocky did manage to get up, he walked away with only a few minor scratches. But I wasn't so lucky. I had three broken ribs, my right leg was shattered with thirteen fractures, and I had cracked my skull. It took me all winter to recuperate, and when I returned to the ranch where I was working my attitude had changed. I knew painfully well now that I was not so invincible after all and I was much slower to assume I could simply impose my will on a horse. Instead, I resolved to watch and listen to it and try to figure out if there was another way. I was looking for something that was a little easier on both me and the horses. This was long before horsemen like Tom Dorrance or Ray Hunt had become common knowledge in the horse industry. I was searching alone in the dark for a better way to work with horses, with nothing to guide me but intuition and desire.

When I look back at it now, this time in Nevada was the start of one the most interesting and productive periods of my life. I was on my own, living in a little camper truck I'd fixed up right near the corrals where the ranch owner kept his string of half-wild horses, many of them actual mustangs with generations of freedom bred into their bones. I was practically living right among them. There were many days—weeks, even—when I spent more time with horses than I did with people. I worked with the horses all day long and often well into the evening. I spent many nights sitting on top of the haystack just watching them by the light of the moon as they interacted in the field—soaking up how they moved, when they moved, and why they moved. The horses were all living together unrestrained in the expanse of pasture, just like a wild herd, and it couldn't have been a better class-room for me to observe natural horse behavior. But more than just watching from the other side of the fence, I also spent considerable time in the middle of them. A big part of my job was to head into the remuda and catch the next horse or horses for that day's work. It's quite a trick to separate a single horse from a herd of more than one hundred. As any horse person knows, if one horse starts to go, pretty soon they're all moving. I'd be in the middle of all that billowing dust and all those flying hooves, trying to do my job but also trying not to get hurt, which was a pretty powerful incentive to watch closely and learn quickly.

As I watched and learned, I got so that I could sense when a horse was about to make a move. I could even tell what kind of move it would be. I could tell which horses were in charge of the herd and which ones were happy to simply follow orders. And I could tell when the horses at the top of the pecking order were preparing to challenge each other. I was learning to read the signs and pick up the clues.

Here is an example of how immersed in horse life I got. When I was in among the herd, things used to get a little too tight sometimes so I'd lift my arms up in front of me and use my elbows to hammer open some safe space when a horse leaned in on me. "Get off me!" I'd curse at the pushy ones, not thinking anything about it. Well, I had a girl-friend at the time and she used to stay over occasionally in my camper with me. One morning I woke up to find her out of bed and down on the floor. When I asked her why she was down there she shot me a cold look and hissed, "You know very well why." I protested, all inno-cence, and when I pressed for an explanation, she said that she'd slid over in the middle of the night and, instead of a warm snuggle, I apparently snarled at her and gave her a good stiff elbow in the chest. Eventually, she forgave me, but she never did sleep over again.

About then, I finally acquired a horse of my own—Quincey Top Cat, or T.C. for short, the first horse I ever bought with my own money. He was a big liver chestnut quarter horse with bright eyes and a snap to his gait that I spotted in a shipment of colts coming to the ranch. With T.C., I discovered something that planted within me the seeds of some crucial insights. My job, in some ways, was pretty much like an assembly line. I was charged with getting green colts ready for basic riding—we called it "green broke"—and it was all about getting the job done safely, quickly, and efficiently and moving on to the next one. With T.C., however, I wanted to try something a bit different. I wanted to take my time. I had a fuzzy notion that I wanted us to be more than just horse and rider. I wanted us to feel like best friends and partners like I did with my dog, Dudley. And besides, after a long day of working green colts into prospective saddle horses, I neither felt like nor had the energy to be in a hurry with my own horse. So I spent a lot of time on the ground with T.C., working with him on a lunge line and in the round pen, studying him and how he reacted to the various things I did. Seeming in some ways more like a golden retriever than your average horse, he was kind, forgiving, and genuinely willing to please. We got along so well that I never had a single bad moment with T.C. and we developed a relationship I'd never before had with a horse. It felt great, and it felt healing. Things T.C. did soaked into me, sometimes on a level I didn't even know existed. I owe that horse so much, much more than I knew at the time. From our start together in the round pen all the way until we were out riding alone, just the two of us exploring the trails above Lake Tahoe, T.C. showed me that there are basically three types of horses: "yes" horses, "no" horses, and "maybe" horses. T.C. was an extraordinary "yes" horse and he was the first to open my eyes to the possibility that a horse could truly be a willing partner instead of a mere beast of burden. With him, I had the confidence to do some crazy things.

One of our favorite games was to ride out into the big pasture where my employer kept well over a hundred head of horses. We'd work our way quietly in behind the herd as they grazed and then we'd explode, break into a full gallop, stirring up the herd as I hooted and hollered, and we'd get them all charging full speed. It's impossible to describe the magnitude or sheer voltage of the thrill you get when riding your horse in the middle of a herd of more than one hundred horses all running as fast as they can. I knew that if something went wrong and I fell off, or if we went down together, we'd probably both be killed or at least seriously injured. But I didn't care and neither did he. We were simply two young males having fun at any cost. The best part of running with the herd was when we would need to jump the huge irrigation ditches that crisscrossed the field. Amid all the dust and horseflesh we were entangled in we could never hope to see the ditches coming. Our only clue as to when and where we needed to jump was by seeing the rising and falling waves of horses ahead of us as they jumped. The herd looked more like a school of dolphins arching gracefully out of the water then splashing back down below the surface. I relied totally on T.C. to get me through these moments and he always did. I still smile when I think about him.

I worked at that ranch for four years. Between my daily immersion in herd dynamics and the regular tutorials T.C. gave me on individual horse psychology, I was getting a pretty good undergraduate degree in equine behavior. Eventually, I had what I believe are two profound insights, insights on which everything I've taught since then depends.

The first lightbulb that went on as I sat atop the haystack was this: horses don't make a distinction between how they feel and how they act. Their physiology is inseparable from their psychology. They haven't learned to divide their body from their mind and their spirit. If they're scared, their head and tail will show it. The same goes for anger, trust, stoic defiance, confidence, and playful aggression. To adapt an old saying, their bodies are the windows to their souls. And because they know nothing different, horses will assume the same is true of us. Horses are simply incapable of understanding that what we humans feel is not always what we show. The idea of laughing on the outside while really crying on the inside is fundamentally unhorselike. An uneasy horse will always show it with a tightly tucked tail and a high head. An uneasy human might show it any way from aggression to nervous laughter. No wonder we confuse horses. We confuse each other.

The second insight I had was that those horses in the field weren't just dumb beasts, nor were they blank slates on which I could scrawl whatever I wanted. As the old saying goes, I could lead them to water but I couldn't make them drink. Horses had an entirely different way of interacting with the world than I did, one that was complex and subtle and supremely well-adapted to the survival of both individuals and the species. Like most profound truths, it seemed almost too obvious to be worth stating. But also like most profound truths, it unlocked mysteries that had puzzled me for years, the way a heavy padlocked chest swings open at the simple turn of a key. And like most profound truths, it can be very simply stated: humans are predators and horses are prey.

Despite thousands of years of agriculture, humans remain hunters at heart. And despite thousands of years of domestication, horses remain prey. It's written all over our respective faces. We humans have eyes in the front of our head, giving us the binocular vision we need to focus straight ahead and accurately gauge how far we are away from whatever animal we're sizing up for lunch. Horses have eyes on the sides of their heads, giving them a nearly 360° field view to allow them to spot a potential attacker.

This distinction between predator and prey, I believe, determines a lot more than our place on the food chain. Predators, for example, tend to think and behave in ways that are fairly linear. We see a goal—a moose grazing in a swamp, a trout rising in a pool, a nice fat, cash-rich corporation just begging for a takeover—and we zero in. We spot targets, focus on them, and move directly toward them. Everything else gets shut out until we make our kill or until the prey is captured or escapes. This is not necessarily an act of cruelty; this is simply how we make our living. We've gotten good at it. In the old days, you didn't eat if you couldn't "bring home the bacon," and although the context of how we go about the hunt has changed, that's still true today, when you stop to think about it. This tendency to goal-oriented, A-to-B thinking is at the heart of what I've come to call predator consciousness. Any time you see someone narrow their range of awareness to exclude everything but the object to be seized, from a wide receiver pulling in a football to a young girl completely wrapped up in cuddling her dolls or a young boy focused intensely on a video game, you're watching predator behavior. I can see it in its purest form out my back window when my cat stalks a bird. Nothing is more important to Haiku than whatever unfortunate robin is in her sights. And when she's finished the hunt, she sleeps, dead to the world. When you're not hunting, you might as well nap. It's not even that she needs to hunt. Her dish is full of food. It's just that predator behavior is hardwired into her DNA the same as its mine or yours.

Compare that to how a prey animal stays alive. Its food—grass, lichen, leaves—is free for the taking, lying all around. What they have to be on the lookout for are predators. And a predator can come from anywhere, anytime. I've used this analogy many times in my lectures, but it's a crucial understanding. If you want to understand the basic psychology of your horse, think about being alone at night in a strange city, walking back to your hotel on a dark street through a dangerous neighborhood. A horse's whole life is like that. While our predatory survival strategy alternates between fierce, focused concentration and complete rest, prey stay alive through sensitive, all-encompassing awareness that never lets up. While we're like the telephoto lens, they're the wide-angle. We think in straight lines, they think in curves and circles. We think on or off, they think in constant awareness. We think about capturing the prize, they think about not being captured. That doesn't mean they just stand around quivering in fear. Horses eat, sleep, procreate, and even recreate. It's just that they have to combine everything they do with a constant vigilance. And their best defense is to keep moving forward. They're like backcountry skiers moving through avalanche country. They'll joke with their friends, stop for lunch, admire the view, and crank some powder turns, but all the while they're assessing the direction and strength of the wind, the temperature, the angle of the sun, the aspect of the slope, and the feel of the snow pack beneath them.

Predator and prey have come up with different solutions to almost every problem. Take, for example, the tough-love, real-life issues of competition and dominance. Both predators and prey travel in groups; both have to come to some sort of arrangement about who's going to be in charge. But predator and prey go about establishing their hierarchy in radically different ways.

For us predators, competition is really an extension of the hunt. Generally speaking, most of us don't go so far as to actually kill the competition these days, but still, we know who's won when one party immobilizes the other. Wolves establish dominance by wrestling until the weaker wolf is on his back, trapped, his belly exposed to his opponent. Submissive members of the pack will even roll over of their own accord, saying in effect, "You're the boss—you're the top dog."

We do it, too. Consider many of our games. In wrestling, the match is over when one contestant is pinned, and in football, they blow the whistle when the ball carrier gets tackled. Rugby, soccer, and hockey are all games where opposing packs fight for possession of the prize, classic predator behavior. When we've got the competition on his back, immobile and vulnerable, as we stand or lie over him, we're saying in the crudest possible predator terms, "You are under my control." It's not cruel, really, it's just the natural dynamics of how being a predator works. The most important thing in a predator's life is being a successful hunter/capturer or being allied with one, and this kind of competition places good hunters in charge. That's what predators need. The logic of hunting informs everything we do.

Prey, however, live by different rules. Their survival depends on the ability to "hit the ground running" and always be ready to move. They flee from predators and they migrate to find food. Even their mating rituals require movement. I can't stress this enough: with apologies to Bruce Springsteen, horses are born to run and this is reflected in how they compete with each other for dominance. If predators play hockey or football, then prey are track and field athletes, swimmers, or tennis players. While predators compete by immobilization, prey (especially horses) will compete by making each other move. In a herd, two horses will sort things out by seeing which one will make the other turn and yield their space. That's what's happening when two stallions rear up and strike at each other. Horses compete to find out which one will turn tail first and allow the other to push him forward. In the crudest sense possible this was what was happening between Stella and the other two mares that ganged up on her and this is also what got so ugly between her and me. I saw this all the time from atop my haystack at that ranch in Nevada, and anyone who has spent any time around horses has seen them compete with each other by pushing each other around.

(Interesting in a sort of Wild Kingdom kind of way, you say, but so what? Well, compare the results of the two kinds of competition. The losing predator has been victimized, belittled, and, implicitly at least, threatened. He has been turned, against his will, into prey. In prey competition, however, the loser has only been forced into doing that which comes most naturally to him—moving. There's no victimization, only the working out of who is most fit to lead, which all members of the herd know has to be done. To make the leap back to sports, I've always found it interesting that the sports most prone to brawls, even total bench-clearing brawls that see entire teams go to war with each other, are predator-style games such as hockey, football, basketball, and baseball. Ask yourself, when was the last time you saw a fight break out at a track and field or swim meet?)

To recap, then, I had developed two insights: for horses, physiology equals psychology, and humans are predators, horses are prey. When I put the two together in the round pen, magic happened. When I began to give the horse what it needed in the language it understood, a channel seemed to open up between the animal and my own deepest heart. I found that if I wanted my horse to be confident and clear-minded, I had to approach it with those characteristics in myself. If I wanted consistency, I had to give consistency. Anything I wanted to create in the horse, I first had to do to myself. I found it was simply impossible to fake it. The horse's prey-tuned senses would read my body language like a newspaper headline. And as I got deeper and deeper into what my horse wanted and needed from me, I began to find resources in me that I didn't know I had and that I was happy to discover.

I found that to get a horse to truly, willingly, follow my lead, I had to convince it that I was worth following. Think back to my thumbnail description of horse psychology. Essentially, it boils down to this: horses are victims that need to move. No matter how big and scary they sometimes seem to be, what's implanted in their genes is fear and trembling. Their deepest need is security. If you give them that, they'll give you everything.

So how do we speak to them? The same way they speak to each other—with our bodies. You can't help doing it, whether you know it or not. As soon as you walk into a horse's field of view, which is pretty close to 360°, you are not only being measured up and read, you are also conveying your own messages. But here's the thing—you're a predator, with predatory instincts. Even if you're a little girl growing up in a new age vegetarian family your body language is still that of predator. I've seen it a thousand times: someone with all the good intentions in the world walks over to an unsuspecting horse and the first thing he or she does is head for the face and pats the nose or neck. The face and neck, of course, are the first places a predator looking to make a kill or simply make contact would go. The message that person has just given the horse is "I am the type of being every cell in you has been bred to mistrust." And the next thing the person does is "catch" the horse by using a rope and halter to immobilize and control the head. More predator-speak. More stress for the horse and more trouble for the rider.

Clearly, anyone who wants a calm, trusting horse as a willing partner instead of just a beast of burden is going to have to unlearn some primitive reflexes and study up on a different way of looking at the world. And in later chapters, we'll get to that.

I want to emphasize that there's much more here than just a system of equine etiquette. Imagine yourself living in the fear-filled world of a horse, where every rock or bush or pile of stuff in the corner of the stall could be hiding a deadly predator. Wouldn't you be looking for someone you could trust, someone who could be counted on to make the right decisions and see you through? That's what your

> horse wants you to be. In fact, your horse wants quite a bit from you. Your horse wants you to be trustworthy, sensitive, and kind. Your horse wants you to balance assertiveness with empathy, consistency with accountability, composure with passion, awareness with proactivity. Your horse wants to know you have mastered the perfect push and that it can count on you to herd it to safety. It wants you to earn its respect, focus, trust, and willingness because it knows you can cause it to move better than it is able to move on its own. It wants you to show it that you can improve its ability to move, coaching it how to run better, faster, and longer, jump higher, stay better balanced, and move with greater flexibility and quicker reactions. It wants you to overcome its own survival instinct, so it can bow to your authority and give itself over to you body, mind, and spirit, because it will consciously realize it is better off with you than without you.

In fact, if you think about it, your horse wants you to balance your

> predator mind with the values of prey consciousness. It wants you to be the better horse. And if you know how to read it, your horse is giving you constant feedback on how close you're coming to that ideal.

This polarity between predator and prey has become the key to how I understand not only my relationship with horses but also my relationship to the world. It's not as big a stretch as you might think. Nature is full of seeming opposites that, in fact, depend on and flow into each other. Night and day, for example. Winter and summer. Male and female.

Humans have been taking the hint and using these kinds of intellectual tools to understand the world almost as long as we've been asking questions big enough to need them. Ancient Chinese philosophers considered the duality of yin and yang so fundamental that they used it to organize everything from their metaphysics to their diet. In the West, we have the grand theories of Georg Wilhelm Friedrich Hegel, who believed that all of history could be understood as the interplay of opposites achieving new and higher levels of synthesis. And ever since Freud told us about the conscious and unconscious, we've been applying this kind of tool to our own psyches. So it's not just me. I'm part of a long tradition, maybe even the longest.

So there I was, with some new and some not-so-new ideas on horsemanship and personal growth and how one could support and enhance the other. I was lucky with my timing—"horse whispering" was becoming a popular media buzzword, thanks to a couple of books and a movie. As I've said, my ideas caught on and I did well. For a while, I was feeling as if everything was going my way. Maybe some of you remember the way my first book ended. I wrote about an idyllic little daydream where my wife and my kids and I would ride off into the sunset at the head of a whole new community of new-school horse people. Things didn't quite work out that way.

By the late '90s, my wife Anita and I were having serious problems. I don't need to get into the reasons why, but it was becoming clearer all the time that our goals were moving apart instead of coming together. I owe Anita so much. It was she who first encouraged me to start thinking about what I was doing instead of just operating on instinct. It was she who pushed me from being a horse trainer with a few unusual ideas to becoming a teacher. And that's on top of the years of love we shared and the two beautiful children we were raising together. But our lives were no longer aligned and we didn't know how to put them back in the groove. We weren't even sure we wanted to. Eventually, we split.

I bought myself an RV and moved into it. I stayed there when I was on the road and when I was back at what was once my home visiting the kids. In some ways, it was like the old days, just old vagabond me, traveling the continent with my house on my back. Like the old days, I had a lot of time to think, traveling between different engagements and lectures. I'd been relaying my message for more than a few years now, refining it and adding to it. I'd seen thousands of students and workshop clients, and patterns were beginning to emerge for me.

Slowly, I began to formulate a new version of my old message. The original inspiration of predator and prey remained at the heart of it, but years of experience and observation had taken me much deeper. I felt I now had a more profound insight into both horse and human behavior, and I felt I had a much clearer vision of where this kind of work was leading. There were eight steps. Each built on the previous one, but at the same time they were all interrelated. Sometimes I thought of them as a ladder, sometimes as a web. Call it a path, I suppose. With a nod of acknowledgment to my Buddhist friends, call it the eightfold path.

[3]

don't put the cart
before the horse

M Y FIRST BREAKTHROUGHS with horses happened back on that ranch in Nevada, when there wasn't anything in my life except them. I had nothing to do all day except work with horses and nothing to do all night except watch and think about them. In a way, although twenty years later, the breakup of my marriage to Anita brought me back to those days.

Long before the time we finally split, I was already working on the road more often than I was at home, and travel like that tends to cut you loose from what most of us call real life. The novelty of new places eventually wears thin, and your world actually shrinks. People drift in and out of your life. The news falls away to an easy-to-ignore background hum. Every highway starts to look the same and the same specials show up on every restaurant menu. Before, Anita had always been an anchor for me, a link back to a place where I was "daddy" and "honey" and I had a role and a place. Now, even though I still saw my kids regularly, that place was gone and that role was up for negotiation. Just as I had been in the old days when I was practically living with the horses, I was cut off from the normal world. The only places that were real to me were riding stables; the only people I interacted with were students and workshop participants. I had lots of "in-between time" to think.

Driving from town to town in my motor home or sitting on yet another plane, I tried to figure out how our marriage had gone wrong—and what it meant that it had. I had been so sure with Anita. I had felt that we were each other's destiny. I could still recall when we met: I was competing at a combined driving event in Carson City, Nevada, on a stormy late summer afternoon. I was hitching up a great little Morgan gelding to a cart when Anita came over to introduce herself and talk to me about a horse she was having some problems with. She tapped me on the shoulder and when I turned around—no lie—a bolt of lighting stabbed down from the darkening sky above us and struck one of the hills just behind her, starting a small wildfire in the sage. It was as if Mother Nature herself was pointing this woman out to me. Within just a few days of knowing Anita I had a dream one night in which I saw two children, a boy and a girl, playing together in a sandbox, and I knew without a doubt that these were to be our children and that Anita and I would start a family together. Sure enough, within just a few months we were married.

I had vowed long ago to follow my visions, and I always had. But it didn't seem to have done me any good, for here I was, alone. Everything that I had thought was solid was now up for grabs as I found myself looking back over some very basic principles. I was trying to come to a new understanding of my own life, especially as it concerned my responsibility as a father to my kids, Raven and Adler. Where I had once seen my path so clearly, I was now grasping in the dark and full of questions.

The heavy workload was almost a relief, for I had plenty of students and clinics to keep me from falling completely into myself. In fact, I concentrated on my work a little extra hard (I had two households to support now) and the forced intensity did bring some benefits. Cut off from the rest of the world by constant travel, living on my own in the motor home, I was completely immersed in my work and the students I was leading. Just as back in Nevada, I had nothing to do except teach students all day about horses and nothing to think about at night except how the problems people had with their horses seemed more and more not unlike the problems most of us encounter in our relationships with each other. Slowly, just as I had once come to understand the patterns in horse's lives, I came to understand the patterns in how my students learned and in how I related to people around me. I realized that, more and more, I was starting off my instruction by talking about alignment.

Alignment, very simply, means this: position yourself strategically. < It's an easy, three-word slogan, but it bears some examination. "Position," as I use it here, means literally just that—where you stand in relation to the horse, how you stand in relation to the horse, and where and how both of you line up in relation to everything and everybody else in your immediate environment. This is your first step in thinking like a prey animal, which means you have to develop a 360° awareness of spatial relationships. Your horse is intensely aware of them. To be properly aligned, you must be, too.

The next word in the slogan is "yourself." I didn't say "the horse," or "the lunge line," or "the horse and rider." Alignment is your problem and your problem alone. Once you're with your horse her happiness is your job, no matter what her state of mind was when you first showed up on her scene. She wants you to be a good leader, but as we'll see, she won't go out of her way to help you. You have to take responsibility—not only for this first step of alignment but for everything that comes after as well.

Most students don't have too much problem with those first two words. If they don't quite get their position right at first, they at least understand what they're trying to do and catch on pretty quickly. And almost all the people I deal with are willing to accept personal responsibility for their actions with their horses, even if they don't really know yet everything that's going to entail. The last word, however, is more slippery. "Strategically" suggests having a strategy, and having a strategy suggests having a goal. You'd be surprised how few people have given this much thought.

Try an experiment with me. Hold your hand over the next paragraph and ask yourself what it is exactly that you are trying to accomplish with a horse when you work with it in the round pen. Or, for that matter, what is truly your ultimate goal when you're training or working with a horse? Take your time. Come up with as many answers as you need until you think you've got the final one.

Most of the people I play this little game with come up with answers like "Join-up," or "Trust," or "Respect" or "Partnership." These are all wonderful things to achieve with a horse and we all hope to get there, but something more fundamental than that has to happen first. The starting point is control. And ultimately, that's what this is about. We are trying to get the horse to accept our leadership and to do our bidding. We want her to do it willingly, even joyfully, but we want her to do it. Alignment starts with the realization that every move we make and every position we take must further our leadership aims.

Control is a tricky issue for a lot of people. I deal with many touchy-feely new age students who are way out of balance when it comes to working with the animal kingdom because they have huge issues with the concept of "tough love." They let their pets literally "walk all over them" (and from what I've seen, their children most often run them ragged as well) because they want to be "kind" and "loving" and "unconditionally accepting." When in a position of authority or leadership people like this tend to reject the whole idea of being dominant and in control as "unspiritual."

I say these people are in denial because when it comes to their horses they conveniently forget just who "keeps" whom behind fences and who assumes to climb on the back of whom and who is going to be in charge of deciding where to go when out on a trail ride. It's all fine and dandy to call this relationship between human and horse a "dance," but let's not forget that somebody needs to lead the dance. There are even authors and well-respected authorities in the horse world spreading the message that they find the notion of control morally objectionable. Maybe they've got scars from being in controlling relationships in the past. Maybe they don't feel they're capable of exerting authority, or maybe they don't feel they deserve to. Other people are simply tired of being in charge of everything else in their life and they just want everything in the round pen to be all sweet and innocent and lovey-dovey. Frankly, control pushes emotional buttons in most of us.

But coming to grips with the need for tough love and control is your next step in understanding prey consciousness. Remember what a horse is: a victim with an overriding need to find a position in a herd with a strong, competent, assertive, and nonthreatening leader that will keep her safe. If you step into the round pen with anything other than the determination to be that leader, you're letting your horse down in the most fundamental way. It's easy to get up on a moral high horse and say we should never have to "hit" a horse, but while you are trying to define your personal limits as to where the line is between "tapping" and "hitting" and then crosses over into striking and abuse, don't forget to take a look at how rough and violent horses naturally are with each other. Be real about how horses actually interact with each other with all their fighting and then try to define what is "right" or "wrong" or "natural" to a horse. I'm not justifying or condoning abuse, I'm simply asking you to recognize the need to make peace with the issue of tough love when you're in a position of authority or leadership.

So what does it mean to adopt a strategy of control? One thing it means is confident, self-assured body language that is definite and not tentative. You'll make mistakes, but you can at least make them boldly. A friend of mine used to be a pretty good trumpet player. Trumpets are loud instruments and when you make a mistake, everybody knows it. But you can't back off while playing a trumpet because being timid just causes you to crack more notes. So my friend's teacher always used to tell him, "If you're going to make a mistake, at least make it a good, loud one." We need that attitude. We need to walk into the round pen as if we're about to play a fanfare.

The other characteristic of a strategy of control is intention. Think about the awareness of prey animals. Their survival depends on not missing a thing in their environment and that first and foremost means you. They will be constantly sizing you up and reading your every gesture, so every gesture must mean what you want it to mean. Every move we make must be part of our overall plan, and every move must be consistent with it. Remember, this is a deadly serious game to a horse. She believes she's putting her life in your hands, so in order for her to trust you, she has to get the same responses and the same messages all the time.

Let's do another thought experiment to drive home how important this issue of consistency is to a horse. Would you fly with a pilot who landed his plane safely 60 percent of the time? How about 80 percent of the time? Would you be happy with 95 percent of the time?

Horses don't have an off switch, or an autopilot. When you're with a horse, consistency is how she measures integrity, so the horse must be your prime focus all the time. She needs your constant reassurance that everything's in control, and everything from your position to your bearing, breathing, and even the subtlest gestures must reflect this. It sounds daunting, but horses are remarkably forgiving. To adapt an old phrase, to err is human, but to forgive is equine. It's amazing how long they'll put up with our garbled gestures and halting approaches. They won't perform very well, but they'll most often put up with it. And it's beautiful to see how generously they'll respond when we get something right. That positive response from a horse builds confidence and enthusiasm in the student and things start to take off between them. Interestingly, when students start to catch on to this, it starts to spill over into the rest of their lives as well. When horses start to see you as confident and competent, it isn't long before everyone else does, too.

In horsemanship, it's often said that forward movement is everything. The quality of that forward movement, however, whether it becomes angry, frightened, confused, dull, suspicious, or calm, confident, and focused, all depends upon the strategic shape and relative position of the leader producing the forward movement. In other words, proper alignment is the foundation of the building, the balance of the bicycle. Everything we talk about after this chapter depends on our being properly aligned. It's appropriate, then, that we spend a little time on the technical specifics of what it means to be in the right place at the right time with a horse.

We've already mentioned the one place not to be—around the head. Even horses never go into this area to herd each other forward, and the reason is simple: that's the first place a predator goes when he's trying to capture the prey or make a kill. This rule is a tough one for predators to follow. Going for the head is a reflex for us to communicate affection as well as aggression. We kiss our spouses and children on the lips and the cheeks. We talk face to face. We even scratch our dogs and cats behind the ears and they love us for it. But I can't emphasize enough that we must stay out of the horse's face. The horse knows you're a predator, so when you enter the round pen you've already got one strike against you. Going straight for the head, even if you're only trying to make nice and friendly, just confirms what the horse already suspects right down to her DNA. You will only create fear or anger, not trust. And then, when we immediately put a halter or a bridle on the horse, constricting her movement, we've compounded her insecurity.

I'm not saying we shouldn't bridle our horses, or be able to spend time near their necks or heads, but there are ways in how we do this that are much more equine friendly. A horse can be left completely stressed out or relaxed and receptive, all from something as simple as how the halter or bridle is slipped over her head. I often compare how we are with a horse to the bedside manner of a nurse or doctor. Let's imagine that you have a phobia about needles and it's time for your annual flu shot, or perhaps you've summoned up the courage to donate blood. Either way, my point here is that if you're apprehensive about being poked with a needle, then how the nurse or doctor goes about the process can affect your comfort level and your willingness to ever go through the process again. Most of us have experienced a careless medical professional who has just simply poked us with the needle to get it over with. It hurts. And we have also experienced those who are attentive and caring, working with finesse and a genuine empathetic "feel" for our well-being in how they go about giving us the needle, and when they say, "There you go, all done!" we are pleasantly surprised at how easy and painless the experience was. Both educated professionals, but the careless and unsympathetic healer validates our fears and reinforces that needles are indeed a bad experience while the truly caring healer helps us see that needles aren't so bad after all. Horses read these kinds of messages in simple things such as how we stand next them, groom, saddle or bridle them, how we lead them, or how we pick up their feet. For the record, I get called in to "fix" lots of horses who nobody has been able to get near with a syringe, and time and time again it is because they have been poked and prodded by people, including veterinarians, with little or no understanding of how a horse reads our body language. Veterinarians, and all horse professionals who are "healers," be they horse-shoers, chiropractors, or massage therapists, all learn how to diagnose what ails a horse but few ever learn the appropriate body language that can help a "no" or a "maybe" horse become a "yes" horse. It's a huge problem in the horse industry—the healers need to heal themselves first.

When you do need to get to the horse's face, take a tip from nature. You don't see too many straight lines in the wild. Natural lines curve, so instead of striding directly to the head, walk in an arc toward the shoulder. Once you're there, press or nudge against a "button" that every horse has down on her girth, low on the ribs, just behind what we might call the "armpit" of the horse. Pressing this button tells the horse to flex her barrel away from you. Once she does bend her ribs away from you her head will swing right around, most likely ending up right next to your shoulder or down in your lap. If you want the head to come to you, push to bend the girth away from you. It's a nice little object lesson in how taking the indirect route to get what you want often yields better results than the so-called direct approach. Simply going for the head is a capturing move that will instantly put a horse on her guard. Remember, straight-line, A-to-B behavior is what predators do.

Alignment is a question of position and strategy. Almost always, our intent is to push the horse forward. This mimics what horses do to each other in the wild and it's the best way to start convincing your horse that you are the leader in this particular herd. To push the horse forward, stand away from her, closer to her back end than her front, with enough distance between you to avoid being kicked if the horse decides to challenge you. Your hips should be open to her girth, with your belly button focused on her shoulder while you deliver some low to level flicks with the lunge whip toward her flanks. There's another button there, a button marked "Go." You press that button by gently flicking your whip or rope in the direction of the flanks, simulating a herding nip from a dominant horse, keeping your core or belly button aimed at the shoulder. You step forward into her space, remaining in this correctly aligned position. As your rope or whip extends from a low to level position, you send an assertive push without "rearing" your whip to become overly aggressive or intimidating to the horse. While the whip says "go" to the flanks, your belly button facing her shoulder is pushing her body away from you laterally, so that the forward movement in the horse is moving away from you, "out" onto the rails of the round pen, instead of turning in toward you. Simply put, while the whip says "go" to the flanks, your core to her shoulder says "but not here."

Your hips are crucial here. Horses take their reading of your body from your core, so that's what you must remain aware of. Almost everybody, including Olympic-level riders, aims at the "go" area in the flanks with their lunge whip but they get way out in front of the horse's shoulder with their core. When our predator instincts kick in, we do not realize that our center is aiming straight at the head of the horse. Despite the forward push from the whip to the flanks, when our hips point at the horse's head, we are signaling an attempt to capture. This is exactly what the horse innately feared all along. Her head will turn away, her barrel or hips will start leaning in or bending back against the pusher/capturer, her hindquarters will most often swing around in a gesture of disrespect and defiance, and her attitude will degenerate into fear, anger, and suspicion.

Inadvertently aiming our core at the head of the horse is the main reason so many of our horses travel a circle in the round pen or on the lunge line "bent out of shape" and stressed out. In fact, even in so-called "educated" training barns all over the continent, there are horses being "bitted up" with side reins so that they are prevented from flexing their necks, heads, and bodies in the "wrong" direction while being lunged. Of course, using mechanical devices to prevent what our predatory body language is causing only stresses out the poor horses even more. Anyone who has spent a little time around the average training barn has seen horses blow up on the lunge line, aggressively rearing, kicking, and bucking while being worked, or bolting and trying to run away. Horses work themselves into a wet lather and even try to escape from the pressure by attempting to jump out of the round pen. People are totally unaware of the fact that while their lunge whip is saying "run away from me" their core is also saying "I'm coming to capture you." It's a classic example of human dysfunction: our own ignorance pours fuel on the fire we're trying to extinguish.

We predators are so head-focused we don't even notice that we are the cause of most of the behavior problems we want to fix in the horse. We're looking at "go," we think, why can't the horse respond to that? But the horse doesn't care about your head. She's listening and responding to the predator intentions of your body language, whether you are aware of it or not.

If you've done it correctly and pointed your hips at the right spot, she'll start moving away from you. But remember, the idea here is to push her forward to establish nonthreatening dominance. If you don't keep up some level of push, she's simply avoiding your authority. You have to keep the pressure up, with your hips remaining in constant position. And you have to keep up exactly the appropriate amount of pressure. Push too little and she'll just saunter around the pen without having learned any respect for you at all. Push too hard and you'll scare her. We want respect balanced with trust, not fear, and the fine line between the two is a razor's edge that varies in sharpness from individual horse to horse.

This is where learning to read equine body language comes in. I guarantee, the horse's body is telling you exactly how she feels about what you're up to. And that will determine how much push or motivation to move you need to give her. It's a bitter pill of accountability that so many horse professionals just refuse to swallow. Be they healers such as the veterinarians or horse-shoers I was just talking about, trainers, riding coaches, or upper-level competitive riders, the fact is that the behavior and performance potential of a horse is a direct reflection of how she feels about what she sees in you, the handler. To a horse, *who* you are is based on *how* you are.

I have to admit, I get a huge kick out of this part of my work. A horse's body is remarkably expressive, with a vocabulary and grammar all its own. Legs, ears, tail, head—they're all saying something. Sometimes the message is unambiguous and sometimes it's subtle, with one part of the body modifying another part the way an adjective modifies a noun. There's probably a whole separate book out there about equine body language, but it's worth introducing some of the basics here.

The tail is a good place to start. There are six basic messages a horse relays with her tail. If the tail is hanging down, softly curled, that horse is relaxed. If it's swishing back and forth, she's annoyed with something (probably with you or the flies). If it's being twirled around, the horse is feeling aggressive and threatening. A tail being held up like a plume says "Yippee—look at me! I'm hot stuff! Let's

CHRIS IRWIN

As Kathryn lunges Geordie as so many people do, with her core area aiming at his head, Geordie reacts with high-headed fear to what he can only interpret as a predator coming at his head. His bulging eyes and stiff tail pointed toward the ground indicate that he is highly suspicious. When a horse lunges like this, it's all too common for the trainer to attempt to "fix" what he perceives as the horse's behavior problems.

CHRIS IRWIN

Geordie immediately relaxes as soon as Kathryn simulates the body language of an assertive but nonthreatening horse instead of a predator. By aiming her core at his shoulder, while using a low to level whip to ask for impulsion from his hindquarters, she is sending a herding message instead of a capturing threat. Note how curled and relaxed his tail has become, that he is stretching his neck nicely, and that he is turning correctly on the circle with very soft contact on the longe line.

play!" If it's stiff and pointing on a downhill angle, that says suspicion. And if it's clamped tight and tucked into the hindquarters, that horse is scared.

Foot position is also revealing. Front feet held parallel, side by side, is called square and means the horse is relaxed and not going anywhere. If one foot is staggered ahead of the other, the horse has only paused and is about to move again at any moment. Pawing the dirt is frustration. I'll talk about the head at some length in a later chapter, but for now it's enough to say it can express everything from the submission of the low-headed bow to the twirling of anger and the fear or defiance of a head held high. When a horse turns her butt to you, that's a sign of disrespect and defiance of the rudest sort. It's how a horse uses her body language to literally send the message "bite me." It's a direct challenge to see if you've got what it takes to come in and push to create movement. If she's feeling not quite so uppity but still wants to make the point, she'll cock a hip in your direction. Sometimes, she'll signal a bit of rebellion by crowding your space, perhaps by swinging her girth into it or pushing into you with her shoulder.

Watch the mouth, too. If she licks her lips, that means she's feeling reasonably okay with you. It doesn't necessarily mean she respects you, but at least she's calm. And a yawn is a very good sign. It has nothing to do with fatigue. A yawn is how a horse releases anxiety or mental tension, and that's what we want.

And of course, each body part has to be read in context with the others, as if it were a part of a sentence. If I had a horse with her head up, a front foot gently pawing the dirt and her tail closed between her legs, I'd say that horse was frustrated about feeling apprehensive about something and needs to be reassured. This horse needs praise and affection more than a push. On the other hand, a high-headed horse who cocks a hip at you with a curled/calm tail is confidently challenging you without being too nasty about it and therefore deserves a moderate push away. A cocked hip aimed at you with a tail puckered up tight against the hindquarters still deserves a push because the cocked hip is a challenge, but the tight tail suggests apprehension so the push must be gentle. Push the tight tail too hard and you'll create more fear. You'll get respect all right, but it's the respect given a bully. On the other hand, if that hip cocks at you with a wringing tail, expressing anger and an aggressive challenge, you had better crack the whip and give that hip a seriously assertive push away from you or that horse will not respect you and will likely escalate her challenges toward you. Again, reading the tail tells us how hard to push. Too hard, we create fear, not firm enough and we'll never earn enough respect. All horses are looking for a leader with the awareness to herd them with the perfect push.

It's a lot to think about, I know. But I can't say enough about the importance of body language. It's all a horse has, and she doesn't understand that it's a language we don't necessarily speak. She just assumes that we mean everything our bodies say, no matter how contradictory we appear. We simply have to learn to take body language seriously. After all, it's an underestimated part of person-to-person contact, too. Psychologists say over and over again that most (perhaps as high as 70 percent) of the true communication that passes between people is via our bodies, not from our words—and the two don't always agree with each other. As the old saying goes, talk is cheap, but actions speak louder than words. Working in the round pen can help make us a little more conscious of what we're saying to our colleagues and loved ones. Let me give you an example.

I do a lot of corporate workshops these days, and I once did a team-building exercise for a client in Ontario who owned a number of fast-food franchises. A sandwich, doughnuts-and-coffee place, hugely popular in Canada. I asked the owner what his biggest problem was and how he dealt with it. "Employee turnover" was his answer, and he didn't really know how to encourage his workers to stick around. I kept that in mind as I began my round-pen demonstration, playing horse with a nice, agreeable young filly, and then I got one of the store managers to come into the pen. She tried to keep sending the horse the same messages I'd been sending, but she soon found out her body had a mind of its own. Whenever the horse so much as looked at her the wrong way, she'd back up. And whenever she needed to make a point to the horse, she'd be way too forceful about it. The horse was getting mixed messages of submissiveness and assertiveness and was growing more and more confused. I explained to her what she was doing wrong, but she couldn't help herself. She had an ingrained passive-aggressive attitude and her body was simply expressing it.

Finally, she was near tears. "This is just like at work," she said. "My staff is always telling me that they don't know how to take me. One minute I'm trying to be their best friend and the next I'm the boss from hell." She wasn't the only one to make personal discoveries that day and it was a fascinating workshop. All the managers who came in to the round pen discovered their bodies were saying things quite different from what they thought they were saying. But eventually, everyone got things worked out and successfully bonded with their horses.

At lunch, we discussed the turnover problem. A fast-food franchise can't realistically expect to keep employees through wages. The industry is just too competitive to pay much more than the going rate. But what might keep good workers around longer is the same thing that kept the horses loyal and following them around the round pen— respectful, clear, consistent communication. You can position yourself strategically with employees just as you can with horses in order to make your work environment so much more user-friendly than working for the competition.

The more experiences like that I had, and the more time I spent in my motor home thinking about the idea of alignment, the broader it got. It's the first step on the path I teach, the place of beginnings, and it's so vital to get it right in all its aspects. Just as we have to determine whether our bodies are properly aligned for what we want to achieve, we have to do the same with our minds and our spirits as well. Time and time again, just like the young restaurant manager, I find that problems with physical alignment most often stem from problems with psychological alignment.

$\mathcal{A}$T THIS POINT, we want to examine our motives. What are we hoping to achieve, and why? These are difficult questions. Ask them of yourself for real and you might get some uncomfortable answers. Maybe you're in the round pen just to show what an in-charge, commanding kind of person you are. Maybe you're there looking for a refuge from a world that intimidates or overwhelms you. Maybe you're a "wounded healer" trying to save the rest of the victims in the world. There are all kinds of answers to this question, but there's only one right one for the horse. If you're not there to make the horse's life better, you're there for the wrong reason. This is not about you, or your students and their needs. This is about the horse. With hard work undertaken in the proper spirit, I believe we can become better people through working with horses. But that only happens when we start with properly aligned motives. So many so-called "behavior problems" with animals are being caused by their dysfunctional leaders. Sounds a bit like family, doesn't it?

It's challenging stuff, probing your motives on this level. The question of whether you're properly aligned can begin to spread like ink on a blotter. Before you know it, you can be asking if you're on the right path at all. And before you accuse me of exaggerating, let me tell you that I've seen more than one marriage end when one of the partners began this kind of emotional work. Because when you think about it, everything starts with alignment. A poorly aligned car won't travel smoothly or get much for gas mileage until the problem is fixed. Try learning to swing a golf club without a few pointers in alignment and you're not likely to get out of the rough. We often hope that "the stars are aligned" when we start on something ambitious. And it's an old self-help cliché that you can't soar like an eagle when you're hanging out with turkeys. One more corporate anecdote: I had occasion once to dine with the president of North American operations for a major global auto maker who had recently transferred over from a rival manufacturer. He told me he did nothing for the first few weeks of his new job except watch the performance of his immediate assistants, taking both their measure and the measure of the jobs they were being asked to do. When he acted, his first move was to reshuffle his executive team to get the right people in the appropriate positions to maximize their potential. Everyone was happier, and the company ran even better. "That was all alignment, Chris," he told me.

I believe my own breakthrough in alignment came when I first got seriously involved with horses. Before then, I'd been pretty much adrift, skiing in the winter and doing a little carriage and wagon driving and stall mucking to keep me going during the summer. But as horses grew from being just a job to becoming a craft for me, everything changed. At the time, I didn't even understand what was happening. I was just following a feeling, a feeling of healing. But from this distance, it's clear to me now what was going on back then. I was getting properly aligned, probably for the first time in my life.

But alignment, important as it is, is only the first step. Once we're in the right place—in our heads and in our bodies—it's time to take action and make something happen.

[4]

hit the ground running

WE HUMANS HAVE a bit of an attitude when it comes to the animals we share this planet with. We take too much to heart that phrase in the Bible about having dominion over the creatures of the earth. We seem to feel that we can do pretty much whatever we want both with and to them, and, historically speaking, any concern about what's good for the animals has come a distant second in our priorities. I'm not so sure that's the way things should be. I believe our relationships with animals should always be governed by respect and compassion. I believe that control over the earth and animals is not some kind of manifest destiny, but a right we have to earn, especially with horses. That's another reason alignment is so crucial. Getting the appropriate physical alignment that communicates prey behavior instead of predator behavior allows us to successfully compete and earn a position of leadership with horses in terms they understand and accept. Getting the appropriate mental and spiritual alignment ensures that we will use the control we achieve in the best interest of the horses—which, I believe, is the only basis on which control over anything or anybody can be justified. You could say that empathetic control is what we're looking for here.

Alignment, however, is just the start. It brings us to the point where we can say "go" to a horse and get consistent results. "Go," however, creates a whole new issue. It's never hard to get a horse to move. Nothing comes more naturally to them. Moving is up there with breathing and eating on a horse's list of priorities. But we're not after just any movement; we're after a certain kind of movement. Movement, like anything else, can be done well or it can be done poorly.

By this time, it should almost go without saying that the kind of movement we want is going to be the back-end-to-front flow of forward movement. Getting a horse to back up smooth and straight is one of the tougher assignments in horsemanship, and even that is based on the quality of forward movement. So when we say "go," we almost always mean "go forward."

I've spent a lot of time watching horses in fields and pastures with no other humans around to muddy the predator-prey waters. It's a practice I recommend, if for no other reason than to admire what is one of nature's most beautiful sights. But it also gives you the chance to study how horses move when there's nothing inhibiting the natural flow of their gait. If you get a chance to spend some time this way, try to memorize how it looks. Listen for the rhythm of the hooves. Try to imagine how it would feel to be riding a horse that was running as if you weren't even there. Hold these thoughts in your mind.

When we say "go," we want our horse to give us the same quality of unfettered, liquid motion she has when we're not around. I always seem to drift into watery metaphors when I talk about going forward. It just seems natural. The best image I can come up with to describe the kind of motion we want our "go" to produce is like the smooth, powerful current of a river flowing over a deep, sandy riverbed. No ripples, no rapids, no resistance; nothing to disrupt the seamless forward movement of energy. We want enthusiasm. We want willing engagement.

Without proper alignment, of course, it's a lost cause. It would be like trying to drive the smooth circuit of a racetrack with the emergency brake on and without knowing how to properly operate a manual transmission. But proper alignment isn't enough. Going forward introduces its own challenges for the rider and its own obstacles to overcome. Most of which originate, of course, right within the rider.

To speak of "creating" nice, clean, forward movement in the horse is a bit presumptuous. The horse knows perfectly well how to move. What we're really trying to do first and foremost is not interfere with her back-to-front impulsion when we're working with her. As doctors say, "First, do no harm." We're just trying to relax and learn how to stay out of the way of what the horse already does naturally. And then, once we "find our seat" and learn how to work *with* instead of *against* this motion, we can use well-developed equitation skills to show a horse how to move with improved balance and even greater ability than it would discover on its own. More on that later. For now, let's start with basics. We need to discuss positioning (aligning) ourselves in the saddle. And when it comes to being in the saddle, the best analogy I can come up with is skiing.

I've spent a lot of time on skis, and I've learned that you can tell at a glance who the really good skiers are by how they stand on their boards. Their bodies are coiled, knees bent, neither standing on their heels nor the balls of their feet but balanced evenly across the full soles of their feet, with their weight just slightly forward. Their hands are always out in front of them. As they fly down the mountain, their shoulders remain square to the slope, facing downhill. This isn't to say a rider should necessarily look like that, but to make the point that a good skier commits his body to the fall line, which is the most direct path (or path of least resistance) that a marble would take if you rolled it down the hill. He's not hedging his bets, saying, "Well, if this turn doesn't work out I can always stop." His body language says "down," as he commits to gravity and the fall line instead of resisting it. If he falls, he falls forward. His turns will leave nice, cleanly carved arcs in the snow. And he'll likely stay in control because the flexed edges of his skis stay firmly pressed into the hill.

Compare that to the beginner over on the bunny run. He's a little uncertain about this whole downhill business. He's nervous about what might happen if he commits to the next turn—he might get going too fast, he might lose control. So he plays it cautious. He leans back a little, shrinking with fear against gravity, putting more weight on his heels and into the tail ends of his skis. He can create sloppy turns, mostly by using leverage from his butt and upper body, but his skis skid across the snow. Not only does swinging his body back and forth across the fall line create a lot of extra movement that slows him down, but it also makes it harder to balance and tires him out. It also reduces his control of the turn. He's skidding on the edge of control, not carving with precision. Anyone who's ever driven on ice knows that a skid is not a situation of control. And when he falls, it's always on his backside.

It's not that the correct turn is beyond the physical capability of the second skier. It's actually harder work and more complicated to create a turn wrong, so if you can do it wrong, you can do it right. The skier's main problem is in his mind. And the root of it is the skier's failure, from fear, ignorance, or both, to commit to the natural law of working with instead of against gravity in his attempt to go forward down the hill.

As you can probably guess, I've seen a lot of skidded turns in riding arenas, figuratively speaking. And yes, the reasons are the same there as they are on the ski slope. Make no mistake, I understand fear. Horses are big, powerful animals. They can hurt us, and sometimes do, a circumstance I know all too well from numerous painful experiences. And up there in the saddle it can sometimes feel like a long way down. As it is often said, it's not getting bucked off that hurts, it's the landing that gets you. A little hesitancy—a lot, even—is the most natural thing in the world. But believe me when I tell you that failure to commit will condemn you to a lifetime of riding the bunny slopes. And it won't reduce your chances of injury—in fact, it will increase them.

Over the years, I've noticed two main patterns with students who are having trouble with forward motion. Both, at their root, are the result of being gripped by fear.

The first problem I call "going fetal." The rider, like a baby retreating inward to a self-protective fetal position, curls his body as tight as he can and still remain on the horse. Some coaches call this being a "backwards rider" because as part of that reflex, his seat bones, seat, and legs all fall out of correct alignment on the body of the horse. His hands come back toward his gut, nervously pulling back on the reins. That, of course, puts pressure on the horse's face, and we should know by now that this will only cause problems. In addition, the horse's spinal column sags like a hammock underneath the constricting seat and legs of the rider. And as the vertebrae crunch together in this inverted or concave shape the head comes up, which in itself makes the horse anxious. All that alignment work, getting the horse to believe and trust that the rider understands her needs, goes out the window as soon as the rider goes fetal.

Going fetal doesn't necessarily have to be dramatic or obvious. Even at the highest levels of competitive riding, a well-trained eye can often see subtle signs of a rider imploding. Even just a little of this "working against the grain" of the horse results in performance and behavior problems such as incorrect leads at the canter, problems with flying lead changes, or less than perfect lateral work at leg yielding, side-pass, and half-pass.

Regardless of the symptom, the root cause is the same. Your horse suddenly realizes, "Hey, there's a great big predator on my back interfering with my face!" At the very least, that smooth, rippleless forward motion is going to be an increasingly distant dream. The other problem riders have with forward is very much like our beginner skier's. Many riders simply lean forward and stare at the head of the horse, like a skier fixated on his ski tips, or they lean back and brace themselves deep into the stirrups with their butts pushed up and back against the cantle of the saddle. It looks they're riding a chopper. Instead of staying on top of things, it's as if they aren't secure in their position as the leader and they're simply letting the horse pull them along like a water skier behind a boat.

First of all, assuming you're on fairly level ground, leaning forward or backward is going to create doubts in your horse's mind about who's in charge here. Second, it throws everybody out of balance. You've just dropped a bunch of great big mental and physical boulders right in the middle of your uninterrupted current and all of a sudden you're paddling through rapids, holding on for dear life. Again, the problem here is caution, born of fear. The rider is afraid to commit fully to going forward. Somewhere in the back of his mind a nervous little voice is saying, "Maybe I should hang back a bit here" and this is transparently revealed through how his body acts and reacts by recoiling against the forward movement of the horse.

Many of us are quite familiar with that voice. It has its place. The voice of caution and sober second thought has probably kept many of the more devil-may-care of us alive. The problem is that it's insidious. We'll never go broke folding our cards and we won't get hurt staying on the sidelines. It's just that the next time out, our idea of what's possible is a little smaller. We expect less from ourselves. Little by little, our horizons shrink. Because we attempt less, we don't "lose" or "fail," so we kid ourselves into believing that our success rate goes up, illusory as it may be. And after a while, we're trying to convince ourselves that pats on the back for second-rate achievement feel just as good as would the ones for something grander.

This syndrome goes far beyond the horse world—far beyond, in fact, the sports world. If we let it, fear of commitment can infect everything we do, from the failure to follow our dreams to the search for true love. We'll be okay, but we'll live in a world where the colors are a little duller and the music is a little muted. I think horses want us—need us—to live differently. They need us to put our whole hearts into it when we engage with them. And if we're successful at it, seeing the amazing results we can achieve with horses will build our confidence and it'll be easier for us to do the same in the rest of our lives. I think one of the reasons horses were put on earth is to remind us, in the words of the hockey legend Wayne Gretzky, that you miss 100 percent of the shots you don't take.

There's one other type of fear that gets in the way of going forward. For many riders who have had enough time in the tack to make their peace with the physical risks of riding this second form of fear doesn't stem from the chance we might suffer actual harm, which is at least reasonable. Instead, it is the fear of looking foolish in front of others. The horse world is full of big money and even bigger egos. There are plenty of people eager to render judgment on whoever happens to be working or performing in front of them. In fact, there are plenty of people like that wherever you go, its just that horses are seemingly magnets for control freaks, ego maniacs, and spiritually arrogant wounded healers. Ego can be a productive force and pride can be an effective motivator, but when it gets out of hand it blocks almost all forward movement. It makes you afraid to make a mistake, which means you're not going to try anything new. If you do make a mistake, you're so concerned about how other people react to it you lose the opportunity to learn from it. And worst of all, ego can completely shut you off to anything new. After all, don't you know it all already?

Fortunately, there's a simple antidote: a sense of humor. It's easy to get swept up in all this talk about being your best self and ultimate communion with your horse and start taking it—and yourself—a bit too seriously. Remember this: nobody worked harder at achieving enlightenment than the old Zen monks of Japan, but they took time ◁ out to laugh, write poems, and get together with their friends for some tea or maybe something a little stronger. I think a lot of us need to lighten up. I know I do. After all, taking something too seriously can be just as damaging as not taking it seriously enough.

Getting beyond inhibiting fear is a big step toward achieving quality forward movement in the saddle. But there are also positive qualities you need to acquire as well, qualities that contribute to realizing a smooth, liquid stride from your horse. You're familiar with

ANITA IRWIN

Chris's son Adler with his father during a clinic in Mexico just a few days after his fifth birth-day. This is Adler's first time trying to bicycle without training wheels and he is feeling sad because without the alignment aid of the training wheels he can't find his balance.

Chris takes a break from working the horses and helps Adler with his alignment and gives him a boost forward.

ANITA IRWIN

With a little help from his dad, Adler is soon balanced, forward, and smiling with success.

ANITA IRWIN

the first one, probably to the point of being tired of hearing about it. But I can't emphasize enough the importance of simple awareness. If she's asked with correct position and alignment, a horse will usually start her forward motion from the hindquarters. Just like a rear-wheel drive car, that's where the power is. It's like a wave that starts in the haunches and back legs, gains force and momentum through the barrel, and keeps rolling forward as the impulsion is released out the shoulders, front legs, and neck, where just behind the head of the horse the wave of forward-moving energy crests. To find the right "seat" on a horse, we have to be aware that that's what is going on. Instead of thinking of yourself as a passenger being hauled along by some sort of four-legged bus, think of yourself as a surfer shooting the curl. That should automatically get you to pay more attention to what's going on underneath you and remind you to sit a little more centered and balanced in the saddle. This is not a technical "how to" book for riding so I don't want to get bogged down with specific details about how to "find your seat." Having said that, if you're serious about improving your riding, I highly recommend that you sit down with and soak up what I consider to be the bible of all equestrian books—*Centered Riding* by Sally Swift. There are far too many coaches out there teaching people to pull on the reins and lean into turns. Sally Swift teaches with incredible insight how a rider needs to be aware throughout his entire body in order get plugged into the saddle so that he can ride his horse from his "center" with a deep and powerful connection.

Then there's empathy. You just have to care enough about the horse to openly listen to what she tells you. If you care about your horse, you will care enough to solve and even anticipate her problems. If you don't, you won't. I can't put it any plainer.

We need to be a little careful about this one, because there's a lot of false empathy out there these days. Many well-meaning people are being misled by so-called horse whisperers and natural horsemen on the clinic and expo circuit showing off with circus tricks like bareback and bridleless rides. So often, while the crowd is applauding the courage and charisma of the rider, the horse is sending very clear body language signals that she's not happy. Personally, I'd rather stay in the tack and make the ride easier and better balanced for both of us with the aid of a well-fitting saddle and correctly used bridle. If you ride for your horse, you can have her flowing forward with a softly curled tail, relaxed back, a soft expression in her eyes, relaxed ears, and a moist mouth with lots of contented lip-licking. Riders in the know call this a horse that is "coming through nicely"—meaning the back-to-front flow of power is fully engaged, uninhibited, making its way smoothly, balanced and elegant, and, if not happy, at least content. I challenge you, no, I implore you for the sake of the horses to look past the illusion of what many in the horse industry carelessly call harmony or partnership and notice what the horses under these riders have to say about what's being done with them. Many are visibly distressed. Sure, it's an appealing notion to think we are closer to nature and more at one with the horse if we ride *au naturel*. But most often with those who do, you'll see their horses are wringing their tail in agitation and pinning back their ears in anger. You'll see the apprehension or fear of a tail clamped tight against the hindquarters—or saddest of all, the blank, low-headed stare of a sullen horse. Pulling off these stunts to impress people while upsetting a horse is the very opposite of empathy.

Empathy's a tall order. It's where I fell from grace and got off the rails with Stella. But with apologies to JFK, I believe we should try to ask not what our horses can do for us, but what we can do for our horses.

You are, of course, the leader in this little two-member herd. That means it's up to you to be assertive. We've already discussed how important intention is to getting proper alignment, and assertiveness is an outgrowth of that. Whether you're on the ground in the round pen, working on the lunge line, leading, schooling from the saddle in an arena, or simply out enjoying a trail ride, you must know what you want and communicate it unequivocally. That, of course, gives me yet another opportunity to harp on the importance of body language. Riders undercut themselves all the time with their body language. I don't know how many times I've seen riders—even the good ones—reprimand a horse by jerking it in the head with the lead rope or reins for stepping into their space after they've taken a step back. When we back up, whether we are aware that we are stepping back or not, we draw or attract the horse in toward us like a vacuum. So when the human inadvertently or unknowingly asks the horse to come in, but then reprimands what they consider to be a "pushy" horse by aggressively using predator body language and tactics such as jerking on the lead rope or chain attached to the head of the horse to send the horse back out and away from them, then these people are essentially getting angry at the horse for doing what they told her to do. What message is the horse supposed to take away from that? This is a classic case of unintentional passive-aggressive behavior. You would probably be amazed at how the vast majority of people, whether they ride horses or not, are completely unaware of the signals their bodies are sending out into the world of relationships. It would be comical if it weren't so sad for the horses. (Let's also not forget about that message from psychologists that body language is how we truly communicate with and evaluate each other. Yikes, no wonder our world is such a mess!)

We've already touched on the value of consistency. Remember, even the biggest and boldest horses are inherently suspicious creatures and they need to be able to depend on their leaders just as completely as infants depend on their mothers. That's why horses test us. They need to know that our responses will be consistent because that means we're paying attention and we understand their worries. To be consistent is to be trustworthy. When we fail, they hold us accountable by sneaking in undesirable behavior, such as shying away from a particular spot in the arena, bending in toward us, or simply focusing their attention elsewhere. When it comes to rebelling, a horse is every bit as creative and stubborn as a typical teenager.

Composure is also important. Most horses can spook at everything from a loud noise to a piece of paper that wasn't there the last time they went around the ring, and when they do, they will be looking to you for reassurance. Stay calm, breathe deeply, stay "plugged in," centered, and relaxed in the saddle, add a little more impulsion to your drive, and stay consistent. That will tell the horse, "I don't have a problem with whatever it is that's worrying you, so it's OK."

Foresight fits in neatly at this point. Look ahead. Learn to anticipate problems. Be proactive. Remember previous issues and recognize when they could recur. A good rider fixes problems but a great rider prevents them. This will be easier if you're practicing awareness the way you should be. (See how this all fits together?)

Finally, a little passion is a very good thing. Horses pick up on positive emotions, too. If they feel your energy and love for riding, they will reciprocate like a dancer happily "swept off their feet." However, if they feel a frustrated control freak, they will rebel.

Yes, that's quite a list. I felt a little bit there as if I were quoting the Boy Scout pledge ("I promise to do my best, to do my duty . . ."), but I really do believe that what happens inside our hearts and minds affects what happens out there with our horses. And your best ally in working on some of these characteristics can be the horse. It's funny, but I've noticed time and time again that horses inspire more effort, perseverance, and dedication from people than we'd be willing to give to anyone or anything else. (There are plenty of husbands of women who ride who can attest to this!) I think it has something to do with how quickly and accurately a horse seems to read our minds. We pick up on that somewhere down deep and we respond, and the more we respond, the easier it all gets. Eventually, working on getting clear, committed, uninhibited movement with our horse becomes almost like a meditative state. And out of this meditative state comes the opportunity to move forward ourselves.

I thought a lot about forward motion in those weeks and months after my encounter with Stella. Things had been cruising along for me pretty well for quite a while by that time. Forward had seemed easy to come by. But meeting that mare had bumped me up against something I couldn't move. And again, my thoughts drifted back to Nevada. I spoke in the last chapter about how aligning myself with horses was such a breakthrough for me. Those horses in Nevada, however, did more than just show me the path. They pushed me forward along it.

I lived a pretty low-maintenance, carefree life back in those days and I tended to stay on the surface of things. If you'd met me, you probably would have thought to yourself, "Party boy. Not much there." That's what I would have wanted you to think, because that's what I was trying to convince myself of, too. Inside me was a tightly coiled ball of pain and anger and hurt. I'd spent a childhood being severely abused and lied to. And when attention and help was what I needed, I was ignored, beaten, or belittled. I'm not angling for pity here. There are plenty of stories worse than mine—I'll tell a few more of mine as we go along, so you can judge for yourself. But growing up was hard enough on me to leave wounds that had never healed. As long as I didn't have to feel anything too deep, I learned to live with my wounds and function perfectly well. But in my heart, I was limping. And I didn't want to admit it.

Then I started getting serious about the horses, thinking about what kind of being the horse is and what I was asking of it. When I fully understood what a horse is and how it thinks, and what it takes for these incredible creatures to give their hearts and trust to a human, it did something profoundly important to me. If a horse can face its fear and move on from the hurts and disappointments of its past, I realized, I could, too. What's more, I had to in order to lead the horse.

I was no longer satisfied with just drifting like a lily pad on the surface of my life. I wanted better. When I look back at it, I know that what was happening was the first stirrings of my desire to resolve issues instead of pretending they weren't there, although I didn't have words for that kind of thinking back then. I knew it would be a long path. I didn't even know where it was going. All I knew was that I had begun something.

I still had a lot to learn, but for the first time, I had both found a way forward and witnessed living examples of the courage it takes to go there with the horses. Of all the gifts horses have ever given me, these may have been the most valuable.

[5]

hold your horses

*A*FEW YEARS AGO, I met a woman—I'll call her Laura—at a big horse expo in Columbus, Ohio. Laura came to me saying she had major problems with her horse, a big, strong, stressed-out thoroughbred that she had "rescued" after the mare retired from a career at the track. I agreed to meet with her and see what I could do.

When we got together the next day, the first thing I noticed was that this equation had not two factors, but three. There was Laura, Laura's mare, and Laura's mother. The second thing I noticed was that all three factors had common denominators. The horse was high-strung, nervous, and twitchy. She was neurotic, demanding in a passive-aggressive kind of way, and constantly all over you and in your face. So was Laura. And so was Laura's mom. Wow, I thought. This would require some delicate diplomacy. Some situations take a while to resolve and an in-and-out coaching job can often cause more trouble and heartache than it fixes. But Laura pleaded with me, saying everyone was advising her to have the horse put down before somebody got hurt. I was her last chance. So I decided to try my best.

It was hard to miss the fact that Laura had a needy and sometimes thorny relationship with her mother. You could see that the older woman had refused to relinquish the hold she had over her daughter, even though Laura was now in her late twenties. Mom was there even during the coaching sessions, reserving her right to approve or disapprove of her little girl's behavior. For her part, Laura seemed to both welcome and reject her mother's persistent appraisal. She was always looking over at her, gauging her reaction, constantly looking for reassurance that she was a good daughter. It was easy to imagine her going through life like this, putting up a bold front of independence, then caving in shortly after to get her mother's approval.

That's certainly how she was with her horse. Laura would try to stand her ground with confidence and be assertive enough to get the big thoroughbred mare to follow her wishes, but she caved in physically and emotionally and backed down every time the horse turned in and challenged her in the slightest. She even broke down in tears when I explained to her that it rudely meant "bite me" when her mare turned her hindquarters to Laura, vehemently swished her tail, and trotted off away from her. It wasn't just unfortunate melodrama, either. That horse (Lola was her name) was packed with as much tension and mixed emotions as her owner—a time bomb ticking, an explosion waiting to happen. Helping Laura with her control issues, I realized, would probably save her from serious injury with Lola somewhere down the road. So, in front of an audience of thousands during a demonstration at the horse expo, I parked Laura outside the round pen with her mother and walked in to work with her horse.

I didn't expect it to take long to establish a bond with Lola and it didn't. She had all kinds of issues and problems. She was all over the place at first, literally bouncing off the round pen walls, and she seriously challenged me a few times. But just like all horses, what she really wanted was someone dependable and consistent who would take charge. That's what I gave her. And when she saw that I was assertive without being threatening and that I wasn't about to back off, she came around. In about forty minutes she was following me around the pen like a puppy dog, head held level and tail hanging loose and easy. She was yawning constantly, letting the anxieties pour out of her, her body, mind, and spirit devoted to my lead.

KATHRYN KINCANNON-IRWIN

In Bermuda, Chris is asked to work with a notoriously pushy and aggressive chestnut mare. Her reputation is to appear "easygoing" until asked to do something. Here Chris has positioned himself and the mare up against a fence to resolve "who pushes whom." He is bending his core away from the mare, indicating in horse language that he is "open" and it is okay for her to turn in toward him. He has aimed his core behind her to make it very clear that his push is working her from back to front. Chris' posture is telling her to move forward and swing her hindquarters "away," which should cause her body to move out and her head to turn in toward Chris. He is carrying a lunge whip in a low/passive pasture so as not to push "too hard." The contact on the longe line is not to pull her head into him but merely to "block" her head from turning out and away from him if she should attempt to be rude and turn her hindquarters to Chris as a threat.

Feeling that the contact on the lunge line and halter is in place and that there is a boundary without a gap (no slack) in Chris' contact, the mare does indeed decide to turn in headfirst instead of threatening Chris with her hindquarters. However, she leaps aggressively into the turn, trying to intimidate Chris and push his contact out of the way by leaping into the air and throwing her head up as high as she can. She is swishing her tail aggressively at him and she is trying to throw a kick toward him with her hind right leg. If you look closely you can just see enough of Chris to notice that he has "folded" his core off, bending at the waist so that his impulsive energy is not "on" and confrontational with the head of the mare as she turns her head in his direction.

Less then 10 minutes after they met, the mare is bowing with total respect, focus, trust, and willingness away from Chris with her body, doe-eyed and relieved to finally meet a human she can understand. Note that Chris is bending his hips away from her head while his core is aiming at her back end. Chris and the mare are bending away from each other as a sign of mutual trust and respect for each other.

Within a few repetitions of this exercise, the mare has seen that Chris is herding her from back to front—without pulling on her head or ever having his core "up and on" when aiming at her head—so she quickly relaxes and becomes level headed, allowing her adrenaline and aggression to subside. Her swishing tail indicates that she is still mildly annoyed, but her stretching spine and soft eyes, ears, and mouth all show how relieved she is to be "herded" by an assertive but non-threatening leader. Note that Chris has his body facing out in front of the mare with his core folded "off" and the whip is held low. Also note that the lunge line has gone totally slack as the mare has no need to turn away from Chris.

As Laura watched me, something seemed to click with her. Laura had seen me do this the previous day at my demonstration with a "troubled" Andalusian gelding, but maybe whenshe saw me work the same changes in her own horse she decided that kind of relationship was possible for her, too. Or maybe she was just tired of the way things had been and finally saw a way out. Whatever the cause, I saw an almost immediate physical change in Laura when she reentered the pen. She wasn't a big woman, but she stuck her little chin out and stood her ground when that mare came thundering up alongside her. She stood up like a traffic cop and set boundaries for that horse and found the conviction in her body language to make sure they were respected. After Laura saw the transformational change possible in her horse, her whole bearing changed from high-strung, ditzy, provisional, and weak-willed into something focused, firm, and resolute. The results weren't long in coming. When Laura first entered the ring, her mare was again all over the place like a 1,200-pound jackrabbit trapped in a cage. The mare had no regard for Laura whatsoever. At one point, Lola even turned to aggressively bite at Laura. But before long, as Laura rose to the occasion, Lola was following her around all doe-eyed and mesmerized. I was amazed and delighted and the audience gave them both a standing ovation. And just as she was leaving the ring, Laura shot her mother a look of mingled triumph and warning. Hmm, I thought, maybe some new boundaries are developing there, too.

Once Laura got a taste for this new feeling, she never looked back. We worked together a few times after that, with Laura and Lola driving all the way up from Columbus to Toronto to take part in my Train the Trainer program. Now I'm very pleased to say that both horse and rider have come a long way. They currently compete at second-level dressage and are consistently in the ribbons. Laura has at long last moved out of her mother's house and has her own place. She began studying martial arts as a way to improve her awareness and ability to control her body and now competes successfully in karate. She's got a new boyfriend and a new job. She's got a new and improved life.

It's been amazing to watch her growth, and it began, at its heart, with a moment of contact with her horse. Contact is what we must work toward after we've got forward movement. After all, once you tell a horse to "go forward," the next issue is "go where?" Just as alignment adds intention to position, contact adds intention to forward. And how does contact communicate intention to a horse? It takes a horse that is "out of hand" and sets consistent, focused boundaries to show the horse the balance and quality of movement, and therefore peace of mind, that comes from being "in hand."

I'm going to return to an image I used in the last chapter. I described the kind of forward motion we want to create in the horse as being like a smooth, powerful current in a river. No ripples, no rapids, just flow. Now it's time to extend the metaphor. If the horse is the river, the rider is the banks. You can't tell a river where to go—water is always going to follow the path of least resistance. All a riverbank does is create the boundary between where it's easy to flow and where it's hard, essentially telling the water where to go by showing it where not to go with boundaries. This is exactly how we create direction with our horses. We tell them, "Go anywhere you want, but don't go here, or here, or here."

"OK," says the horse, "I'll go over there." And that, of course, is the direction we want, the one direction we've left open.

Imagine you're riding your horse in the direction from six o'clock straight up to twelve o'clock. Your right rein shouldn't be used to pull right toward one o'clock; your right rein is to block the horse from turning left toward eleven o'clock. Conversely, your left rein is not to pull the face of the horse left toward eleven o'clock; it is to block the horse from turning right toward one o'clock. The hands don't pull to steer the horse to twelve o'clock, they only hold to create boundaries that block the horse from turning away from twelve o'clock. Our contact is used first and foremost to channel the river of the horse to focus movement by blocking all unwanted turns away from a specific direction.

There's a story I like to tell from my early days in Nevada about the importance of creating boundaries. I find men consider it particularly convincing.

My second wife, Robin, used to have a lovely horse named Emerald Bay that she, frankly, spoiled a little. Robin was constantly slipping Emerald little treats, especially carrots, that she'd feed her by hand. It got so that Emerald came to expect a carrot—or whatever you happened to have in your hand—pretty much any time a human was standing nearby. Emerald would come pushing right into you looking for a handout, licking her lips and chomping her teeth, whether you invited her in or not. I was riding Emerald up in the mountains one beautiful sunny afternoon when I dismounted to admire the view of Lake Tahoe far down below us. Forgetting all about Emerald's nasty habits, I took the opportunity to unzip my pants and relieve myself. Emerald, much to my surprise, greedily swung to chomp into her expected treat, and I swear I damn near lost my carrot! Ever since, I find you just can't say too much about the importance of setting boundaries.

Like everything else when we're dealing with horses, contact must be established right from the start and must be kept up until a horse learns how to "carry itself"—a concept we'll talk about later. For now, if we've got training to do, it's not time for a free rein. Instead, as soon as a horse steps forward, she must step into contact. Most riders hold the reins too slack or too tight, which gives the horse no focused definition at all. You have to tell her, and keep telling her, where the path of least resistance is. If you don't, you've given the horse too many choices, a selection of confusing options to choose from instead of just one path or "open gate" to follow. You'll immediately lose her attention, and her focus will start wandering, the way a riverbed splays out all over the place as it approaches the ocean.

Stepping into contact, however, is a subtle thing. You don't want the horse to feel that you're slamming a door in her face as soon as you ask her for forward. Before you start setting boundaries, you have to meet the horse's forward, advancing energy with your own absorbing, receptive energy. It's like pushing a kid on a swing. You don't simply wait until the swing is at the apex and then shove away at it. Nor do you stand there in its path and wait for it to hit you. First, you gently catch it on the backswing, absorb it into a momentary pause at the apex of its swing, and then gradually start pushing until you give it a big boost into the next cycle. It's a yin-and-yang sort of thing (interesting how these dualities keep resurfacing, isn't it?).

I find that my students grasp the "feel" for this kind of contact when I take them down out of the saddle and ask them to climb in next to me while I drive a harness horse in a cart or carriage. It's amazing how people lighten up and relax when they're sitting on a wagon instead of in the saddle. And when I hand them the reins, called "lines" when driving, they're able to find their ability to absorb and hold the movement of the horse much more easily and quickly because they're not nearly as prone to going fetal when they are in the cart as they are up in the saddle. Once they know what it feels like to have "a horse in hand," I ask them to mount back up into the saddle, and with their newfound sense of feel they soon have a horse that is visibly more relaxed and fluid in her movement.

As Ray Hunt says, it should be the horse pulling on you, not you pulling on the horse. Another analogy I often use is that of waterskiing. It's a common reflex for people when they are learning to water-ski for the first time to try to pull themselves up and out of the water instead of letting the boat do the pulling while they simply hold the handle of the tow rope and absorb the impact of the pull throughout their body. When novice water skiers respond to instinct and try to pull their bodies out of the water they always fall forward and crash over the tips of their skis. However, when they learn how to simply hold and absorb the movement as the boat pulls them out of the water, then the fun begins and they are up and riding the waves in no time.

The idea of absorbing energy is useful in all aspects of working with a horse. In the round pen, for example, we absorb the horse's forward movement when we take a couple of steps backward in order to get in front of the horse to stop her or turn her in to us as she comes around the circle on the rails. If we are moving forward instead of backward when we get in front of a horse, we are two forward moving energies that are apparently about to collide "head on," and this really stresses a horse out. However, when we are walking backward or retreating to get in front of a horse, we are allowing space to absorb them into a halt or turn. When riding or working on the ground with ropes or lunge line, absorbing energy is also expressed through our hands with the gentle but firm use of the reins that "catch" the mouth of a horse instead of capturing it. Here's what I mean: If I throw you a ball, you'll reach out and "catch it" with absorbing energy as your hands retreat toward you to absorb or soak up the forward movement of the ball. We withdraw our hands and arms into ourselves with retreating energy to absorb what we are catching (when it is already coming to us)—like a ball thrown in our direction. However, just the opposite, like a cowboy throwing a loop in his rope at a steer, we reach out with advancing energy to capture what is moving away from us. As I said earlier, how we go about catching a ball is the opposite of how we capture a butterfly. Catching requires retreating to absorb what is coming in your direction while capturing requires advancing to seize what is trying to avoid being captured. Unfortunately, dysfunction ensues between so many people and horses because we are innately hardwired to want to advance to horses to capture them instead of drawing them in to us to catch them. Would you trust or willingly give your all to anyone who has to capture you in order to work or play with you?

We haven't talked much yet about the role of the contact between a rider's hand and horse's mouth in riding—or any kind of work into a bridle—but now it's time to bridle up. Both the halter and the bridle are properly used to establish boundaries for the horse and get the horse "in hand." That doesn't mean you turn a horse with the reins. To repeat: Your hands absorb forward movement in order to set boundaries for where the horse shouldn't go. Like skiing, turns are created from the core of your body into the body of the horse, and we'll get to that in a later chapter. For the time being, remember that a horse is not a bicycle and the reins are not handlebars.

By now, you can probably guess why that is a no-no. Using the reins to turn a horse means that you're using capturing energy instead of absorbing energy. You are taking the head to establish control of "where to go." That is predator behavior and all of a sudden you become the enemy. The instant you use the reins to steer a horse, stress starts building in her mind. As the resistance in the mouth, head, neck, and shoulders of the horse affect her spinal column, physical distress leads to psychological reactions from fear and anger to stoic defiance and sullenness. All of sudden, your smooth river of horse-power is more like a choppy torrent full of whitewater and boulders. Everything, all the way back to alignment, falls apart.

Forget the whole notion of the reins as some sort of leathery steering wheel. Think instead of an old phrase that originated in the horse world: "well in hand." What do we mean when we say something is well in hand? We mean that it's "under control," it's progressing favorably. We have the sense that something is proceeding at a pace that isn't breakneck, but measured, appropriate, and satisfactory. We need to bring that useful little phrase back to where it came from.

To explain how we get a horse well in hand, I'll return yet again to my well-used metaphor of the river. I've already described the rider as the banks along the river, but that's not the end of it. The rider also has to act as a bit of a dam, or rather, a weir—a low wall that's just enough of a barrier to build up some water behind it without creating a big, sluggish reservoir. That means that as soon as the horse steps forward, she should stretch from back to front and slide into the bit like a hand moving forward into a supple, open, absorbing glove. She should fit into your hand like a glove and know it's there, elastically blocking her from getting ahead of herself and taking off at her own pace, but no more than that.

What's happening is this: the horse's "go" begins in the hindquarters and rolls forward like a wave. But when it gets to the bit, it's blocked from forward, not pulled back, so the horse is held back just a tiny bit. You don't actually need to slow the horse down. She's now working harder from behind, more engaged, more cycles per second, but not faster. What changes is that instead of covering a set distance in twenty strides, she'll take perhaps twenty-four strides. If you're doing it right, you're compressing the horse's spine, coaxing it to bend upward in a powerful curve. Think of a sprinter in the blocks before the hundred-meter race. His back, too, is curved and coiled with powerful, yet supple muscles. When the starter's pistol fires, that collected power explodes into forward movement. The difference for us is that we don't necessarily want to lose that slight compression we've created in the horse's spine. It has something like the effect that high revs have in an engine. It creates a certain nimbleness and gymnastic ability in the horse, allowing it to turn, stop, spin, and jump like a highly trained equine athlete, the way gearing down as you enter a curve improves the cornering ability of a sports car. Football players understand this as well. Watch a running back weave through a defensive line: his strides are short but his knees reach high and come down with the driving power and agility he needs to dodge tacklers and the thrust to brush off the ones who grab at him. Football players actually practice this gait, through the time-honored drill of running through a series of car tires placed on the ground.

I have to admit that these are difficult concepts to grasp without working them out for yourself on the back of a horse. The difference between using your reins to set boundaries for your horse and using them to steer is like the difference between reaching out to capture a butterfly and drawing in to catch a ball. Horses, as we've looked at, understand advancing energy as something coming to catch them. Most riders don't understand this distinction, at least not while they're in the saddle.

There is one concept that's commonly discussed in the horse

industry that starts to address this issue. Coaches talk about "forward riders" and "backward riders." The backward riders always look as if the horse is pulling them along by the saddle. They're always reacting to what the horse is doing, as often as not by pulling on the horse's face. In the language of the previous chapter, they're the ones who are skidding through their ski turns. The forward riders, on the other hand, are going with the horse. They are proactive about setting direction. They are elastic—elastic in the sense that they're like a bungee cord, which only lets you fall so far (you hope)—but firm at the end of the line.

Of course, the backwards riders are going to have bigger problems than not just being able to create appropriate contact for their horses. They won't have quality forward, either, and quite likely will be out of alignment. I'm presenting the concepts in my little eightfold path as if they are all linear, one-after-the-other steps like climbing a staircase, and so they are. But at the same time, they're also interrelated. It's not as if you master alignment and move on to forward, then on to contact after you've mastered that. Working on forward will refine your ability to create good alignment, which will feed back into forward and then into contact and, in turn, all the other steps we've yet to talk about. So while these skills are like a ladder in that you have to have some sense of alignment before you get anywhere, they're also like a web. I've just presented them in this step-by-step fashion because that's the most practical way to explain them in a book.

A big part of establishing good contact and learning to become a forward rider is relaxing your body enough for it to feel and understand the horse's motion underneath it. For the sake of convenience, I've been talking about a horse's motion as if it were as uncomplicated and direct as the flight of an arrow. That's not true, of course. To be sure, horses move forward, but it's a much more complex motion than it looks. It's like a note played by a violin. To our ears, it sounds like a single pitch, pure and beautiful. But if you play that violin note into an oscilloscope and break it into its constituent parts, you'll find that note is composed of many different overtones. They all blend together to create one sound.

In a horse, those "overtones" are the subtle lateral and diagonal shifts that result from the horse's natural gait. The strides go forward, but they also go diagonally side to side as the horse shifts its wave of impulsion and balance from where it starts in the left hind to where it comes out in the right front and vice-versa from right hind forward and out the left front. We'll talk later about how this more nuanced understanding of equine movement affects what we do on the horse, but for now it's enough to know that it's happening. Our seat on the horse and our hands on the reins have to become elastic and flowing enough to ride with the diagonal changing wave of impulsion from back to front, without losing the overall sense of rhythm and flow. Or, as my musician friends might put it, we need to ride with a bit of swing.

In a very real sense, working on contact with a horse starts to define our relationship with it. It's one thing to establish the basic parameters such as who pushes whom, or who motivates movement. But contact begins to address our ability to give the horse focused intent through boundaries. Horses, as I've said before, are more than willing to be led, they're born to be led. When they find a leader they can count on, it's often a huge relief for them. Setting boundaries for a horse, however, is no small thing. What we're doing is taking the energy of a thousand pounds of horse, moving both forward and side to side, and channeling that energy into a focused tunnel that is only as open as the four- to six-inch width of a piece of steel tube—the bit in the horse's mouth. I've never driven a bobsled, but I imagine that trying to keep a sled on course as it hurtles down an icy run feels something like what we're trying to do.

What I'm building up to is that if we're trying to add focus, direction, and intent to the horse, we'd better possess it ourselves first. We need to know what we're doing and what we want, and we need to know it every moment we're in the saddle. There's no time for second-guessing with a horse. She'll sense it in your body language the

Chris in Nevada training "Red," a thoroughbred x quarter horse, for a future in endurance chariot racing in the early 1990s. Note the softness of the contact on the driving lines as Chris channels Red straight ahead with boundaries from the bridle.

instant the question is asked in your mind. If you're lucky, she'll overlook her leader's momentary indecisiveness. More likely, her attention will start to wander. After all, "forward" is only movement. It doesn't say anything about forward to where, and a horse is easily worried and distracted. At worst, you'll cause your horse to start wondering about your ability to lead. You might start getting a few challenges—a barrel bent in opposition to your leg, a sudden reluctance to move up against a rail.

That doesn't mean that we should be inflexible. A leader has to adapt to changing circumstances and a good leader does it before the circumstances start to create problems. But we can't let indecision cloud our contact with the horse. From moment to moment, she has to know exactly what's expected of her if she is to remain focused. And the more concentration and focus we ask of the horse—and boundaries by definition create focus—the more of both we have to find within ourselves.

Sometimes, the boundaries we need to create are within ourselves. It's called self-discipline. I thought a lot about self-discipline during the weeks after my battle with Stella. Maybe things had gotten so out of control in that round pen simply because my self-discipline had broken down. I thought about the personal boundaries I'd crossed holding my own against Stella, and my mind went back to one of the most difficult challenges I'd ever had with regard to living up to my own standards of appropriate conduct.

My ex-wife Anita and I didn't come together under easy circumstances. In fact, both of us were married to other people at the time. When we left our spouses to be together, we both caused a lot of pain for people we had once loved. And the move we made to be together did not improve our social standing in the small Nevada town where we were living. Those factors would put significant pressure on any new relationship, but there was more to come.

Very soon after we got together, Anita became pregnant with our daughter Raven. I'd been thinking about moving for some time, but when Raven came along it became abundantly clear that it was time to move back to Canada—both for professional reasons and, frankly, for the Canadian health care (medical insurance for a freelance horse trainer is a financial oxymoron that was way beyond my reach). So we moved back to very near Swift Current, Saskatchewan, where I had gone to school, with the dream of eventually setting up some kind of program where horses and humans could get to know each other.

The first couple of years back in Canada were tough. It took a while to establish myself, yet I still needed to support my family and get my business going. During our first winter back in the great white north, I took the only job I could find, in a tannery, dealing with raw animal hides coming in from the abattoir. Drenched with blood and covered with bits of clinging flesh, I had to scrape off the wasted meat and body parts and salt the hides that would then be tanned after they dried. Mostly, they were cattle. We'd get the occasional deer, antelope, or coyote. All day long, sun or snow, I'd be up to my elbows in the blood and stench of death, saying a sad and silent prayer of thanks and blessing over the remains of each and every animal that I "processed." Then it would be home to look after the horses. It sounds horrible, nightmarish, and it was. But beggars can't be choosers and soon there was a second child, our son Adler, born on the coldest day in Saskatchewan history.

It would be an understatement to say it wasn't a difficult situation, and for the first time in my life, I couldn't run. People were depending on me and I had to stand and deliver. I did, but the emotional marathon of sleepless worry and effort brought out bad things in me, characteristics I recognized from my past and thought I had left behind long ago. I grew short-tempered and Anita and I had long, hurtful arguments as the emotional wringer of fatherhood took me by surprise. I experienced all kinds of flashbacks from my own childhood, and they tormented me and filled me with doubt. I was terribly worried about being able to provide for my family, too. By the spring, people were bringing me plenty of horses to work with, but they were all either green or difficult, and when you're constantly working with challenging horses it's only a matter a time before you get hurt. Where would we be then, I wondered? The stress started to get to me and I began to lose patience with the horses. If a horse so much as bumped into me it would take every ounce of self-restraint I could muster to keep myself from going ballistic and unloading my anger on her.

For angry I was. I'd always followed where I felt the spirit told me to go, and look where it had got me. I felt trapped and betrayed. I recall one bitterly cold Saskatchewan night with the clarity of a hallucination: I was out feeding the horses in the minus 40-degree dark, facing into a slashing wind, screaming out my frustration to the icy stars: "Why have you brought me here?" The stars, of course, declined to answer. I was stuck, left to my own devices. The only thing I could do was bear down and force myself to keep going. All I had was a flickering candle of hope for the better and my fragile sense of self-discipline. I don't think I resolved any of the anger I was feeling, but I learned a thing or two about my ability to set personal boundaries of where I would or would not allow myself to go. No matter how unbearably hard it got I vowed that I was never going to lose my temper and physically lash out against my family or the horses in my care. That strength and conviction of that vow was tested so many times, but it was never truly broken until I met Stella.

Learning to create boundaries doesn't come overnight. Some people go through their entire lives constantly being pushed around by others. Some worry way too much about fulfilling other people's expectations of them, allowing their parents, their friends, or their coworkers to set their direction. There are a lot of people who'd be much happier if they'd just learn how to tell others when it's time to back off. We all need to set boundaries for ourselves, points past which we tell people that we're sorry, we've chosen to go in a different direction and they need to respect that.

We all need to learn to set boundaries for ourselves, as well. Many people never accept this crucial lesson in life, and as I found out with Stella, you can never assume that you're "there" and that your self-discipline is carved in stone. Sometimes we just have to tell ourselves that achieving certain goals rules out certain behaviors. The obvious examples are athletic—I'm guessing there are few marathon runners with pack-a-day cigarette habits—but there are myriad others. If you want good grades in school, you can't stay out late and cut class. If you want to stay in a fulfilling marriage, you can't fool around on your spouse. Don't think I'm just moralizing. I've taught thousands of students, and in my experience, people who can't set boundaries in their relationships or for themselves can't set them for their horses, either.

At least at first. That's why I started this chapter with Laura's story. Unable to set clear and consistent boundaries with her horse or anyone else, she had no true meaningful and productive contact with either. With her horse, however, she was willing to learn how to proactively communicate boundaries, and the experience carried over and transformed the rest of her life for the better. That's one of the magical things about the relationships between humans and horses—how often these wonderful emissaries from nature can help us help ourselves as we learn to develop the skills they need from us. Sometimes I wonder who's training whom.

[6]

strike while the iron is hot

*E*VERYBODY KNOWS THERE is a right time and a wrong time to ask for something. Kids know when their parents will be most susceptible to that birthday wish. Mom and Dad know when to approach each other for a favor, too. For comics, waiting a beat before dropping the punch line usually gets bigger laughs than plowing on through. And in politics, the art of timing is often the difference between winning and losing elections.

So it is in the horse world. Now that we've got our horses to the point where we're asking things of them, we have to talk about when to ask. If you time your requests wrong, you're just setting yourself up for failure. Not only that, getting the timing wrong makes things awkward and even dangerous for the horse. Your horse will read that as a lapse in awareness and judgment. You've let her down a little and damaged the trust you've been working toward. As the old truism goes, timing is everything.

Good timing, for horses and for everything else, can be defined very simply. Perfect timing is when you achieve the maximum result from a minimal message, the precise moment when you get the most from the least. That means you have to time your request at the instant when the horse is both most receptive to it and is in the best position to do something about it.

Whether your horse is receptive or not is, or should be, in your hands. We've talked about the importance of focus since the first chapter of this book, and as you've probably guessed by now, it's still important in the case of perfecting timing. These skills are cumulative, and every step in this path is important to every other step. So first, we have to get and hold our horse's attention by earning the right to lead through being the better horse. Then we have to give her the kind of leadership that allows it to ease its worried prey mind through constant awareness and consistency. If a slip in your awareness costs you your horse's attention, she most likely won't be willing and able to hear your request no matter when you say it.

In fact, timing is largely a function of awareness. We've already discussed the horse's gait in the context of establishing good contact. The rider has to be relaxed enough to swing with the diagonal sway of a horse's back, but he also has to be present enough to be in the moment with the rhythm and in control of it. Now we need to take that awareness one step further. Proper timing is all about making your requests at the point within the horse's diagonally swinging gait when it's the easiest for the horse to accommodate them.

Probably the closest that humans ever get to experiencing movement something like the four-footed gait of a horse is when they're out gliding on the snow on cross-country skis. The ski poles help propel the skier forward, and so, in a sense, become our extra pair of legs. In fact, just as horses move diagonally, classic cross-country skiers work on something they call the diagonal stride. Maybe you've done it: the skier pushes off with his right leg and his left ski pole at the same time, then alternates to the left leg and the right ski pole. It's basically an exaggerated, more muscular version of the natural way we walk along and swing our arms. The effect, once you've gotten comfortable on the skis and into a nice rhythm, is of a pleasant back-and-forth stride, where the movement of the right leg is balanced by the left arm and vice versa.

Now, imagine you're skiing along a good, straight, freshly groomed trail. You're striding along in a solid groove and gliding nicely when you spot a tight right-hand corner coming up. Now, if you begin your turn to the right when your right ski is forward, you're going to lose your balance and probably wipe out and you're going to wind up in a heap on the snow. That's bad timing. A cross-country skier learns pretty quickly to time the start of a right turn for when he's bringing his left ski forward. Swimming a front crawl is a similar movement: Your arms and legs move in a diagonal relationship as you find yourself facing right as you reach forward with your left arm and facing left as you reach forward with your right arm

The issue with horses is similar. Horses move like swimmers, skiers, or skaters, in a series of alternating diagonal lines. They go forward from right rear to left front, then left rear to right front. How exactly they do it varies from walk to trot to canter to gallop, but that's the basic idea. The spine actually moves in a serpentine shape like a snake or a fish. Asking for a right turn at the precise moment your horse is putting the majority of her forward-moving weight and balance on her left foreleg is the moment of perfect timing and balance for the turn. Not only will she be better balanced to push forward into the turn, she'll know that you truly know how to aid and facilitate her movement instead of causing her problems. If you make the same request for a right turn when her weight is on her right foreleg, she probably won't fall—unless you've made this mistake on slippery or very poor footing. But she'll take note. You've just asked her to cross her ski tips. To her, it's a failure of awareness: "Can't you see I'm out of balance and this is not the correct moment for what you've asked of me?" She won't like the fact that you've let her down, stressing her mind by stressing her body, perhaps even putting her in danger. Someone needs to be leading this dance between horse and human. To expand upon that metaphor, as many a woman knows, if her partner can't lead, she'll take over and lead for him. Poor timing often results in horses taking over and leading the dance with their riders.

CHRIS IRWIN

Kathryn Kincannon-Irwin simulates the diagonal balance of a horse. Here she has pushed her weight forward from her left "hind" leg and has the majority of her weight balanced on her right "front" leg. In this position she is balanced to turn left but she would most likely hurt or injure her right knee, or at the very least lose her balance and fall over, if she attempted to turn her body to her right.

CHRIS IRWIN

During a clinic in Maryland, Kathryn demonstrates a picture perfect right turn with Orion, a young Dutch warmblood gelding. Note that both Kathryn and Orion are initiating the right turn while balanced on their left (Orion's fore left) leg. Also notice that Kathryn is not pulling the turn but instead blocking pressure with the lead rope to tell Orion not to turn away from the track she is indicating with her core. Also notice that Kathryn is aiming her core just ahead of Orion with a little bend in her body away from his head during the turn instead of allowing her core to be aimed into his head or neck. With the diagonal timing that allows balance and Kathryn's core in the correct alignment, Orion is able to flow with balance and enjoy a deep low-headed stretch that fills his mind with endorphins. His tail is perfectly curled and relaxed indicating there is absolutely no stress in his mind or body. He is mesmerized by how Kathryn is handling him!

Think about a football receiver running a pass pattern across the field from left to right. If the quarterback gets the timing of his throw wrong, the receiver might have to reach behind him to grab the ball while he's running forward. Not only is that awkward, it's risky. That's how players twist knees—especially if they get tackled while their body is torqued around. Quarterbacks who throw too many such passes aren't popular with receivers and soon find themselves traded.

(Try this little exercise: Stand up and take a step forward with your right leg. Now push the majority of your weight forward from your left (hind) leg on to your (forward) right leg. Bend a little at the right knee so that you're comfortable and balanced from left hind leg forward on to your right leg. Now, leaving your legs and feet exactly where they are, try to turn your chest and shoulders to the left. This should feel reasonably easy and balanced for you. Now, without changing your leg position, rotate your trunk the other way to the right. Do this on a soft surface because you may just fall over! Now imagine being a horse moving along at a fast pace and having someone do that to you.)

I learned this lesson the hard way when I got all busted up while racing Rocky, the thoroughbred horse I tumbled down the mountain with back during my wild and crazy days in Lake Tahoe. It was this lesson in diagonal balance combined with the neglected need for contact to create focused intent that got us in trouble and caused Rocky to trip. Essentially, I suddenly twisted my torso to look over my left shoulder, with no blocking support from the bridle, and while I twisted left Rocky must've been standing at that same fraction of a second on his left forehand during the gallop. We somersaulted off the shoulder of the sandy path and tumbled a very long way down the side of a mountain. I had the next six months in recovery to think about that one!

There are, of course, more variables involved here than just horse and rider. Let's go back to our ski trail, and this time as we approach the turn we notice through the leafless trees that there's another skier coming toward us who's going to hit the curve the same time we are.

We have to time our turn to allow him to have enough room to also make the turn. Or perhaps the trail stays nice and straight, but we look ahead and see a tree branch that has fallen on one of the tracks. We have to time our stride so that we can lift one ski up and allow the other to glide past the obstruction. Try running up a flight of stairs, leaping and landing on every second or third step, and you'll find your mind and body making automatic fine-tuning adjustments of timing and length of stride.

In other words, we have to think about more than just us. Timing on horseback involves awareness not only of the horse but also of the environment you're moving through. I can't tell you how many times I've been in an arena and seen an educated rider who should know better suddenly pull hard on his horse's mouth because he was staring at the head of his horse instead of watching where he was going. The rider suddenly found himself stressing out his horse by yanking on the reins in order to avoid hitting another horse who had a rider "riding blind," doing the same thing. Timing means both awareness of the here-and-now and preparation for the what's-to-come. And don't forget, you're a part of this horse-and-rider unit as well. That means you have to be just as aware of your own body's movements as you are of the horse's. If you've ever ridden a tandem bicycle or been the passenger on a motorbike, you know how important it is that both riders lean into the curves at the same time.

There's another way to think about timing that we need to discuss. Sometimes timing is about knowing when to ask the horse for something. But sometimes it's also about knowing what is an appropriate request at a particular time. It's important to realize that the total menu of everything your horse can do isn't always available to you. In addition to being aware of your horse, your environment, and yourself, you have to be aware of any limiting factors coming into play. Limiting factors can be either internal or external—for example, you should know your horse's physical condition and should never ask her for something that would aggravate an injury or push her beyond what she's safely capable of. Whether it's too big a jump too soon or a quick canter across ground full of treacherous footing. Again, your horse might try to deliver for you, but she'll be asking herself if you really do have her best interests at heart. Once she asks that, you've lost her.

In fact, few stages in a rider's development are more fraught with frustration and peril than getting timing right. The right request at the wrong time or the wrong request at the right time creates stress in a horse and stress creates reactions in a horse that are immediate and physical. Her back is likely to stiffen up and her head is likely to rise. Right away, she's inverted, and that's going to ruin any sense of quality contact and clean, relaxed forward you've established. And the psychological effect of those physical movements—which we'll discuss shortly—is going to force her to question the very bonds and alignments that you've worked on together. Bad timing does more than prevent us from improving. It actually sabotages what we've already accomplished. Bad timing can cause everything to go south in a hurry. Your car doesn't care if you mistime the clutch and the shift lever when you're changing gears. Your horse, however, cares intensely if you're clumsy and awkward. To make matters worse, she doesn't even care if you timed nine out of ten turns to perfection. It's the one that wrong-footed her and popped her clutch or ground her gears that she remembers, resents, and worries about. And when I say "she remembers," keep this in mind—the memory of a horse is second only to that of an elephant.

When we talk about communication with a horse we're riding, we're usually talking about using the reins to block unwanted turns or to collect a little bit of the forward momentum. But we can also use well-timed rein work to actually create something like a massage to release tension in the jaw, poll, neck, shoulders, and back. Correctly aligned hands with consistent blocking contact that know how and when to offer a massaging type of flexion with the bridle can very quickly sedate and settle down the most intensely volatile horse into a well-balanced partner flowing with endorphins. The full description is a bit technical for this book, but it's a great example of how versatile a tool timing can be when it is done well. The riders who do use timing this well are the riders known to have "feel" or "great hands."

Please don't think that I'm going on and on about timing merely as a means of avoiding wrecks with horses. The same applies when we're training at the most advanced levels of horsemanship. In fact, it's a bit of a cliché in the horse world to say that the cause of problems at the highest levels of equestrian performance can be found as a subtle gap or misunderstanding somewhere in the basic fundamentals of riding. For instance, there's a correct timing and rhythm for when to use your inside leg to work with your horse's alternating diagonal swing when you ask for a leg yield or side pass. It's the same with your outside leg during a half-pass. There is also a precise moment of knowing when to get the easiest upward transition from walk or trot into a canter.

I've come to believe that a truly deep grasp of timing is one of those abilities that is largely innate. You either have natural "feel" or you don't. It's like rhythm—not everyone has a feel for it. Even among musicians, players who have a gift for putting the beat right "in the pocket," as the phrase goes, get special respect among their peers.

But still, everyone can improve. It just takes a lot of time and focused effort. And after a while, it becomes instinctive. Pretty much all the lessons of horsemanship need to be internalized, but timing benefits more from being submerged beneath the level of conscious thought than most. After all, when you get the knack for timing, riding a horse becomes like a dance. The merest suggestion of pressure applied at the perfect moment from a skilled dancer is enough intent to let a woman know where she's going to be led across the floor.

And as most guys probably know, you can't flirt with a pretty woman on the dance floor if you're busy counting ONE-two-three, ONE-two-three to keep from stepping on her feet. Just as a skilled dancer can turn his attention to his partner, developing a feel for timing on horseback to the level of instinct allows you to change your focus from simply trying not to damage your relationship with your horse to trying to deepen it. And that's when it becomes magical for the horse.

Knowledge assimilated that deeply does amazing things. Like groundwater far below the surface, it often flows out again a long way from where it seeped in. Working on timing and the many-pronged awareness that it requires has the potential to change us in ways that go far beyond the riding stable. We become more aware of relationships, both physical and emotional. We become more deft, moving through the world gracefully and confidently. We learn to sense how others around us are feeling and adapt our behavior empathetically and time our actions and reactions to get the best results for all concerned. We schedule the tasks and set the goals that are best suited to the day. We stop fighting our circumstances and learn to work with them, the way a good skier picks a downhill line that conforms to the natural fall line of the mountain. That's not to say that all schedules and requirements should become provisional and up for negotiation. Sometimes, things simply have to get done now even if they're inconvenient, unpleasant, or even risky. But to repeat once more, timing is the art of maximum result from minimum message. Knowledge is power, and if understanding perfect timing can help us achieve our goals, why wouldn't we want to learn?

In fact, in the big picture, timing is crucial. We all have dreams; we all strive to achieve the goals we've set for ourselves. At some point in our lives, the timing will be right to go after those achievements.

I first formed the dream of starting an institute to pass on what I've learned about—and from—horses way back when I was still living in Nevada. When the notion of horse whispering began to percolate into the public consciousness in the late '90s—as romanticized as that version of the myth was—I knew it was time to move. The Hollywood version wasn't quite what I had in mind, but it was close enough to give me a chance. During that entire first winter back in

Canada, whenever I wasn't at work I started writing columns on my thoughts about horse training as a personal vision quest and began sending them off to regional magazines.

And it turned out my timing was good. Magazines were interested in what I had to say and I started to get published. Based on those columns and the national awards I'd won in the United States, I was able to drum up a few clinics, too. By the time the snow was off the ground—granted, the snow leaves late in that part of the world—I had gigs lined up in three provinces. I won't claim that riding horses taught me how to time my business moves, but it did teach me the value of recognizing the moment and seizing it for all it's worth. Like the farriers say, we have to strike while the iron is hot.

This is a long way from the round pen and may not seem like it has much to do with horses. But again and again, it's been my experience that when I learn something about horses—or should I say, from horses—that knowledge echoes out through the rest of my life like a shout down a mountain valley. I'm not alone in that, either. There's something in these magnificent creatures that opens us up to new possibilities. It's almost as if whenever we're working with a horse, her reactions are mirrored in a tiny twin deep inside our soul. What we do with her, and what we ask of her, we also do and ask of ourselves.

We began this journey with me behind the wheel of my motor home, on the road and on my own. Unmoored from the anchor of home through divorce and cut off from everyday routine because of my intense travel schedule, I was able to focus on my students the way I had once focused on horses. I found, just as I had with those wild mustangs back in Nevada, that riders also exhibit behavior patterns. I've learned, I think, that most riding problems stem from incorrect—or nonexistent—understanding of some basic concepts, concepts that have as much to do with our attitude toward ourselves and the world as they do with how we approach the horse. We're about halfway through those concepts right now, and you've probably noticed a few patterns of your own.

For instance, no matter which concept I'm talking about, the word "awareness" comes up over and over again, and I don't know how many times you've heard me insist on the need for calm. And I just can't seem to quit talking about how important it is to maintain boundaries in order to create focus, both in yourself and your horse.

There's a reason I keep cycling back to these themes. At the center of this book—at the center of everything I've tried to teach for the last decade—is a vision of a truly productive and healing relationship between human and horse. This relationship recognizes the difference between the two and acknowledges that someone is going to be in charge. But I believe that if humans earn the right to lead by giving their horses more of what they need from us than they can provide for themselves, the relationship becomes closer to partnership than domination. I believe that if humans study what it is that horses need from us, it will force us to come to grips with our own dysfunctions and balance the contradictions in our nature. And I believe you could replace the word "horses" in the last two sentences with "other humans" and it would be just as true.

Horses live in a world of constantly ringing alarm bells. If they could read newspapers, the headlines would all be three inches high and warning of imminent and deadly peril. The novelist Tom Robbins could have been talking about horses when he wrote, "The world situation is desperate as usual." Your job is to quiet this. Your job is to create a space where you and the horse live totally in the moment, for and through each other. That space is aware, calm, forward flowing, and focused. Every concept in this book is an ever more refined way of achieving that. First we must achieve it in the round pen and with our groundwork exercises. Then it has to happen in the saddle. Then it has to happen as we go through ever more complex tasks. But everything we do with our horses has to return to that same space, the way a symphony returns to the home key or a ship returns to its home port.

We are now at a turning point. Everything we've discussed so far has been fairly physical: how to approach a horse, how we want her to move, and how we use our bodies to communicate with her—or totally confuse them, as the case may be. Now that we're up and in the saddle and at least thinking the right way about what the horse is doing, it's a good time to discuss what the horse is—or should be—thinking.

[7]

level-headed

I'VE ALWAYS HAD a special feeling for the racetrack. I had some of my first experiences with horses at the track, when I was just starting out by mucking stalls at Longacres in Seattle. Being in tight quarters with those big, high-strung animals taught me some of the earliest lessons I learned about being around horses. And when I realized that despite their obvious power, they had been left scared and victimized or angry and sullen most of the time, I developed the deep affinity and identification with horses that has never left me. My time at the track marked me forever.

The track has a similar, if less intense, hold on the imagination of our culture at large, I think. Just look at the impact it's had on our language. So many of our common phrases and images—"photo finish," "down to the wire," "first out of the gate"—have their origin in long barns, manicured dirt, and a grandstand. One of them is the title of this chapter. We may not think of level-headedness as an expression from the racetrack, but it is a key equine physiological and psychological concept.

Remember that horses are incapable of making a distinction between how they feel and how they act. That means that the horse's body language is like a closed-circuit TV link to what's going on inside her mind. Not only that, the physical behavior of a horse is linked to her emotions in a constant feedback loop. Put simply, the way to the mind of the horse is through its body, and if you change how your > horse is shaped and moves, you change, for better or worse, how she feels, thinks, and behaves. If we understand that, we can use that knowledge to further cement our bond with the horse. And from the rider's perspective, the most easily analyzed and influential part of the horse is the head. I've written before that if you control a horse's hindquarters you control her heart. But if you want to read that horse's heart, look at the position of and gestures coming from her head.

There are four basic shapes or "top lines" of her neck and head that a horse can use to express herself. High-headed while inverted, low-headed, level-headed, and high-headed while "rounded." High-headed and inverted (or "hollow") causes the most problems, so we'll start there.

We've all seen a high-headed horse. Ironically, a horse holding her head up high has become a positive symbol of an independent spirit in our popular culture, suggesting pride and noble defiance. There's defiance there, all right. But to someone trying to build a relationship of trust and establish a leadership position with his mount, that's not welcome. When the neck and head of a horse comes up above level with its withers (that small hump that joins the neck to the shoulders), the back is forced to scoop down. The spine becomes hammock-like, or significantly lower in the middle than at both ends. This shape is what we mean by hollowed-out or inverted.

Several things happen to an inverted horse, none of them good. Earlier, we discussed the power of a rounded back, comparing it to the power of a sprinter's body coiled in the starting blocks. But an inverted back is the opposite of a rounded back. As soon as the head comes up and the back hollows out, the power and balance of round is gone and the hindquarters have been robbed of their drive. Your horse, to some extent, will be pulling herself along by her front legs instead of pushing herself from the rear. Even worse, an inverted back causes the horse to brace her entire body as if expecting to run into a wall, with predictably disastrous consequences for confident contact with the rider and smooth forward motion.

Try another little physical experiment: stand up, arch your spine to invert your lower back, and tilt your head back with your chin pointed up into the air as far as you can. Now try to lift one of your knees as high as possible. How stable and powerful do you feel? Do this near a chair, so when you start to topple you'll have something to grab. Now try just the opposite. Look straight ahead. Relax your spine so you're standing with a straight and relaxed lower back (the same as level for a horse). Now lift the same leg and notice how much higher (longer stride) you can comfortably extend from your hip and how much more balanced you are.

As if the loss of power and balance weren't enough, consider what high-headedness does to a horse's state of mind. A high head creates an inverted spine, which causes the horse's vertebrae to pinch together. When that happens, the horse's spinal column starts producing adrenaline and sends it rushing into the brain. The body's logic is that if my head is up, it might be because I suspect a predator is near and I need to be braced for attack while I look around for it. If a predator is near, I need adrenaline to spur my body to run hard and fast. Adrenaline has its place, but it creates a nervous, skittish, angry, or defiant horse. The more paranoid the horse gets, the more likely she is to keep her head up, which causes more adrenaline to flow and the cycle perpetuates itself. And a horse in that state is unlikely to give you the calm, focused awareness that is the foundation of everything we're trying to achieve here.

Instead of that, a high-headed horse is displaying fear, anger, or obstinate defiance. Although there's almost always something that sets the horse off in the first place, those emotions become self-generating in a kind of feedback loop amplified simply by how the horse carries her head. Head position not only indicates the problem, but is an integral part of it. And high-headed, inverted horses have lots of problems.

Interestingly, there are many people in the horse industry who maintain that a certain amount of high-headedness in a horse is good and even necessary. Some jumpers, for example, say that a horse needs to hold her head high so she can read the course and "scope" what it's being asked to leap over. Some of my colleagues in both western- and English-style riding, as well as those working with the gaited breeds such as Tennessee Walkers and Peruvian Pasos, also maintain that high-headed and inverted are the way to ride. There are more than a few rodeo events where you'll find this school of thought as well. These are the horses that are always leaning their noses heavy and hard against tie downs, running martingales and standing martingales. Ironically enough, these are also the horses that are usually involved in speed events.

I don't buy it. Yes, horses do need to hold their heads high to scope out the jumping courses, and many of the breeds do indeed work better while "high-headed." But far too many trainers seem unable to make the distinction between high-headed and inverted and high-headed and rounded. We'll talk about this high but rounded neck later on. For now, it's enough to know there are two types of high-headed horses, high and hollowed or high and rounded. While high and hollow is essentially hell on a horse, high-headed and well-rounded not only allows a horse to look farther ahead but can also feel heavenly for both the rider and the horse.

Don't believe me yet? I challenge anyone riding inverted horses in speed events such as barrel racing, roping, pole bending, three-day eventing, and jumping to spend a day at the racetrack. Thoroughbreds are typically the fastest horses around. Sure, most of those wound-up thoroughbreds will be galloping around the track inverted, full of adrenaline, perhaps braced against their jockey and posturing to each other as they run for the roses. However, the very best horse-and-jockey teams will be able to work together to relax and "stretch out" through the topline of the horse, becoming level-headed as they push for the finish. Those are the ones that will always find that extra burst of speed to win. Track records are seldom won by inverted horses, and level-headed horses almost always pay off in the long run.

In the wild, horses will naturally hold their heads high with an inverted spine, filling their brains with adrenaline, and for a very good reason. They live as vulnerable creatures in a dangerous world. But with us as their benevolent leader, they shouldn't really need to hold their heads up like this—and, if we do our job correctly, we can convince them of that. A high head with inverted back robs their hind legs of power just when they need it most. Besides, high-headedness is simply not a pleasant state for the horse to be in. In fact, it's just plain hard on them. Our whole intent here is to get the horse to do what we want of her own free will by showing her that following our orders actually allows her to feel more comfortable and confident, and following our lead is therefore in her best interest. Constantly stressing them out by allowing, (or even worse, inadvertently creating) high-headed riding isn't going to accomplish that.

The opposite of high-headedness is, of course, low-headedness—or what coaches in the know call "long and low." A low head is a much more positive sign. When a horse lowers its head, the dreaded hollow spine disappears and its back naturally lifts and rounds. This causes the spine to stretch out, and when a horse's vertebrae stretch out, her spinal column starts to produce endorphins instead of the dreaded adrenaline. These are the body's own pain-killing, feel-good chemicals. They help the body keep functioning in case of injury. In humans, endorphins also flow in less dire situations, producing sensations from "runner's high" to the slight buzz enjoyed by lovers of spicy foods.

In the horse, her body is feeling, "If my head is down and my back is relaxed, there must not be any danger." Safety is good . . . let the endorphins flow.

This, of course, is how most horses would prefer to spend their entire lives. And in most cases, it's reasonably easy to lead them there. You just return to first principles to ease their worried minds. Show them that you're empathetically in charge, that you're assertive and consistent, that you're looking out for them and they've nothing to fear. Drive them forward, speaking clearly in their own language, herding them until they're convinced you're the better horse. If we have learned to ride with seat, legs, upper body, and hands that stay out of the way of interfering with the natural back-to-front diagonal flow of impulsion and instead actually accentuate this movement, their heads will lower and the endorphins will bring magic to the horse. For the horse, it's just like falling in love. Or at least like getting a really good professional massage. As their backs slowly round up and their necks start to release down, you can see the negative energy melt away from them.

Low-headed horses are calm and relaxed. That's a great improvement over angry, fearful, and defiant, and getting a horse to lower her head is always my first strategy to deal with most behavior issues. A long and low horse can and should be a vital part of stretching or warming up for any horse and it's also a much-needed transitional phase for horses who have only worked inverted. A chronically inverted horse who has worked with a hollowed spine for most of her life (and there are far too many of them out there in both English and western barns) will need to spend a significant amount of time enjoying the physiological benefits of stretching her vertebrae while moving in a long and low frame.

Having said that, the other side of this truth is that there are only a few games out there, such as cutting cattle, where long and low suits the work at hand. That frame allows for the cutting horse to swing on her haunches for easy and balanced rollbacks and turns while cutting cattle, and the low head keeps the horse athletic but calm, which can also have a contagious calming influence over the cattle. (Yes, an inverted, stressed-out horse prancing around will often do just the opposite and get the cattle worked up and worried.)

However, a horse working with a low head, while very mellow, is not in the best frame of mind for speed, agility, or to be asked to leap over a big fence. Calm and relaxed isn't necessarily where we want to be, either. Just because a horse is calm doesn't mean she respects you—or, in fact, wants anything to do with you at all. This isn't good enough. We want calm and relaxation, but we also want athleticism and focus. We want the horse's undivided attention, and a low-headed horse is simply not in that frame of mind. In fact, if a horse spends too much time in this position she can actually become sullen and unsocial, like an indulged teenager who spends too much time up in his room playing video games. There is a time for long and low therapy and there is a time for a level-headed work. Low-headed is really just a transitional phase, a warm-up to loosen muscles and get into a calm, work ethic sort of mindset before moving on to the more difficult gymnastics.

You've probably guessed that what we're aiming for is somewhere in the middle—level-headed is what we want to start with and is a definite requirement before we try to move to the next step of high-headed while "collected." Somewhere between the stress and dysfunction of the hollow back and the serene complacency of the long and low head is the happy medium that is the truly level-headed horse. Like a contractor building a house, we must take the time and painstaking measures to make absolutely sure our foundation is level before we begin building.

I define level-headed in a horse quite precisely: a horse is level-headed when her poll (that's the especially vulnerable spot on the head right between the ears) is held even with her withers (the hump-like area right above the shoulders). If you want an exact mental image of level, think of the image of the galloping horse that is used as the logo for the Ford Mustang. That horse is running fast but level-headed (I always liked mustangs). That definition doesn't leave very much room for interpretation. Going back to the carpenter and the building analogy, level is either precisely level or it is not. But level is a very specific physical state; and, as we've seen, that means it creates and corresponds to a specific psychological state as well.

Calm is, of course, part of it, but there's much more to level than simple calm. It's a clean slate, a state of relaxed poise. It's a state where there's as little static in the horse's brain as possible, where your message will come through loud and clear. It's the mental foundation that has to be laid before you build anything new. As long as a horse is level-headed, she is learning how to learn. I think of level as a kind of mental neutral, where the engine's ticking over nicely but has been neither revved nor engaged. The goal is for you to engage it and rev it up as you see the need.

The round pen is a great place to begin to work on level. When you've played enough horse games empathetically and correctly to get your horse willing to accept you as leader, she will bow to you with a long and low topline. When the horse respects and trusts you enough to willingly offer her head in this way, you can then take contact with the halter or bridle and begin playing more complex games with the horse "in hand" to show her how your touch can prevent adrenaline and produce endorphins so that it truly feels wonderful to work with you. The horse feels so much better with you than without you. At this point, we want more than just to get her to follow us around the round pen. That's an important step, but it's not enough. We want our horses to be so fixed on us, so focused and confident and totally trusting in us that it's like we've mesmerized them. The state we're looking for is when their minds are blank of any desires except for the ones we've put there.

The method, of course, is always the same—the old game of push-or-be-pushed, be-the-better-horse. But it's no longer enough just to have the horse trotting around the fence. You have to step up your horseplay. You have to get the horse to bend, turn, and change direction, to accept your boundaries as they move in and move out. You have to totally take charge of the horse in an empathetic manner. It's no longer enough to ask one thing, then another thing a few moments later. Your body language has to be speaking in a constant, unceasing flow of lucid commands. You have to assume control of the horse's every move. When your horse realizes that she'll miss something if she loses concentration on you for even a moment and that that's when she feels worse instead of better, then you'll have her concentration at every moment. Horses realize that respecting, trusting, and focusing on you leaves them feeling great, while challenging you or being distracted from you is when they start to fall apart and feel vulnerable. It's like Ray Hunt said: we're "making the right thing easy and the wrong thing difficult." When you achieve that, you've got your horse mesmerized. And chances are, you've found level.

What you're looking for is a specific type of movement, whether you're in the round pen, on the lunge line, or in the saddle. I always compare a well-balanced horse to a train on a set of tracks. No matter whether the tracks are turning right or left, going uphill or down, the train's wheels always stay the exact same distance apart—perfectly aligned on track, as I said earlier. A level-headed horse's hooves are like that. They always remain balanced on parallel tracks. If the tracks turn, the train bends smoothly and evenly around it, just as a horse's barrel and entire body should bend smoothly around a corner. And like the headlight at the front of the train's engine, a horse's head should stay resolutely in the middle of the two tracks, facing squarely ahead.

That last point is crucial. Always remember that the horse has a paranoid need to look around for those nasty predators. She'll take any chance you give her to turn her neck right or left. And in order to look around, she'll usually raise her head in an attempt to go up and over your boundaries. Or the head of a horse will suddenly leave a balanced position within alignment and look left because the rider left an opening in the slackness of the right rein. As the neck suddenly veers left, cause and effect dictates that the entire body of the horse falls off track to the right. Simple physics: Given the long length of an average horse, if her neck swings two inches off balance to the left, her body—especially her hips—"derails" as much as two feet off track to the right. These situations create a sudden loss of balance, a moment of vulnerability and increased stress, and static in the mind of the horse. Enough such moments, enough stress, enough static, and your message is no longer getting through.

We have to keep the head focused on the exact track ahead of us, and we need to be able to accomplish this without pulling on the reins and acting like predators going for the throat to gain control. Ironically enough, the riders who pull the most on their horses are usually the ones in the most denial about what is really going on between them and their horses. These "I don't believe in contact" riders tend to throw away their reins and let them hang sloppy and useless all in the name of being "kind" to the mouth of their horse. I've seen it happen more times than I can count. A rider will start out reasonably well with a horse while riding with no contact, but it never lasts long, because the horse will always feel that paranoid need to look and wander around. Without even realizing what he is doing, the very same rider who has sworn off contact as "bad" for a horse will indeed have a reflex to grab the reins and pull in order to straighten the neck of the horse to "fix it" and place the head back facing in the direction the rider intended to go. All of a sudden the rider is sending impulsive energy into the head of the horse by pulling on the reins instead of using boundaries, like the banks of the river, to block the head of the horse from going where he didn't want her to go in the first place. His instinct to pull on the head is buzzing around in the face of the horse like an annoying hornet. The horse feels predatory behavior and immediately becomes inverted and starts pulling back against the hand that is pulling against her. An escalating challenge of tug-of-war ensues between the hand of the rider and the mouth of the horse all because the rider resorted to reactive pulling to steer the horse back on track instead of using proactive boundaries to block the neck of the horse from turning off track in the first place. A light presence of consistent preventive boundaries is far more user-friendly to horses than a rider with no contact who, as far as the horse is concerned, suddenly changes his mind and strongly pulls to fix what could so easily have been prevented. It's like leaving the gate to your pasture open and then roping and pulling your horses back in after they have innocently wandered out, only to leave the gate open and go through pulling them back where you want them again and again. Learning to ride with a feel for perfect contact is making sure that all your gates are firmly closed except for the one and only opening you want your horse to find and go through.

Having said that, however, even if you did use your reins to proactively block unwanted turns, that doesn't guarantee that your horse will not test those boundaries to see if they are consistent, somewhat elastic, yet firm and resolute. Most of us have seen horses pawing at fences and gates, pushing into them to see if they are solid boundaries or if they can be pushed open. Like a pushy salesman, a horse is not necessarily going to take "no" for an answer easily, but the appropriate prey-like response to a horse testing the channel-like boundaries you are trying to create with your contact is far different than what most people coming from a predator-based mindset think.

If your horse does push through your boundaries and swings her head off track, and you want her attention back, you do it by pressuring the girth on the opposite side of the direction she's looking. That girth will most often bend away from the pressure and swing the head back to where you want it. If you want the head to go from left to straight, then give a little push to the body on the right side, behind the right shoulder, either down low on the girth or back at the hip. It's a little bit like steering a canoe—you don't aim the front of the canoe by paddle strokes from the bow. If you want the canoe to turn left, you push the stern of the canoe gently to the right as you paddle the whole boat forward. In other words, if you have taken all the slack out of your reins and your horse is pulling on your right hand as she tries to look left, do not listen to your instinct to pull back against the pull you feel in your hand. Instead of getting caught up in a game of tug-of-war with the right rein, just hold the right rein firmly and use your hand, arm,

KATHRYN KINCANNON-IRWIN

During a clinic in Bermuda, 16-year-old Brooke Dolan is having trouble with Ocean, her thoroughbred mare. The mare is extremely inverted and she and Brooke are locked up and braced rigidly against each other. Ocean has issues with going into the water and she is visibly stoic and defiant as Brooke rides her into the puddle. Aside from being inverted, also note that Ocean has her ears turned back stiffly, she is pulling hard on Brooke's hand, and her stiff tail pointing on an angle to the ground indicate that she is guarded and suspicious about allowing Brooke to ride her through the water.

KATHRYN KINCANNON-IRWIN

Chris teaches Brooke how to steer Ocean from her core instead of her hands and how to use the bridle to massage the inverted spine and tension out of Ocean. Within minutes Ocean is going level headed and bending beautifully. Notice that Ocean now has her ears relaxed and forward and the reins are much softer as the horse and rider no longer pull against each other.

KATHRYN KINCANNON-IRWIN

Within ten minutes of starting out so inverted and stressed, Ocean is now beginning to carry herself fairly well rounded, soft in the bridle, ears forward, and tail relaxed and curled. The water is no longer an issue as Brooke is creating balance and endorphins with Ocean instead of stress and adrenaline.

After just a few more minutes of coaching, Ocean and Brooke enjoy being able to stretch "long and low," totally relaxed with relief while riding through water.

shoulder, back, and seat to reinforce the blocking boundary you are trying to create with your right rein. Let your horse lean against the wall you have built with the right side of your body, but do not pull. Now, while you're firmly holding the right rein without pulling, just think for a moment where the barrel/rib cage of the horse must be bending if the horse is determined to turn left. That's right. While your horse is trying to look left, her body is bending into or against your right leg. So, while firmly holding the right rein without pulling, it is now appropriate to use your right seat bone and entire leg to push or herd the body of the horse off your leg. As the horse gives to your push and straightens her body, the neck will, as a result, straighten along with the ribs. Simply put, a horse pulling on your right rein to turn left needs to be pushed off your right leg instead of being pulled on harder and harder with the right rein in an attempt to straighten. The same, of course, goes for the left leg if a horse is pulling on your left rein.

But be careful here! There are plenty of passive-aggressive horses who have been hardened by people who pull on them and they have accepted, to one degree or another, being pulled around by the face. However, when someone who speaks horse comes along and starts pushing their girth to get it to bend, these horses will flex their neck in your direction with a vengeance. Try to bend a horse from the girth before she is bowing to you because she likes how you push her around and you may get bitten or kicked. Horses feel that respect is earned from hind end to front end and some will let you know in no uncertain terms that you have no business asking their ribs to bend if you haven't yet established that you can get them forward from behind and turn them from their hips. However, ask a horse who bows to you because it sees you as an assertive yet nonthreatening herder and a little girth pressure gets her straightening and/or bending throughout her entire spine beautifully, with no resistance whatsoever.

If you can't bend your horse to turn her, you haven't established respect, trust, or leadership. What's sad about this all too common problem is that if you can't bend the horse, then there is only one way to turn her and that is to pull on the reins. I should also probably say here that there are two schools of thought among trainers on this subject of how to use contact. There are many, many trainers out there— and some of them are the biggest names in the business— who believe that the bridle should be used to steer a horse. However, ask yourself this: When was the last time you saw a dominant horse walk up to the head of another horse and bite into its face, taking a firm hold, and then begin dragging that horse around by the face in order to get it to go where it wants it to go? It just doesn't happen. Dogs, predators that they are, don't hesitate to pull each other around by the throat, but not horses. Now, on the other hand, when was the last time you saw a horse nip another horse in the body? Look closely and you'll see that a horse doesn't pull the face of another horse to turn her to the right. Instead, one horse will herd the right side of its other's ribs with a nip or a nudge and this in turn herds her to the right. What I'm getting at here is that pulling a horse by the face to steer her is very upsetting. It's counterintuitive to the prey animal, and the first thing to go when a horse is upset is any chance of working or remaining level-headed.

I've made it a bit of a cliché in my kind of horsemanship that whatever we ask from the horse, we must first ask from ourselves. That is never truer than when we start asking for level.

It should be clear by now that horses are always sizing us up, reading the messages our bodies send whether or not we're aware of sending them. When we come to them and ask for level, we're asking for the ultimate in focused, quiet, clear calm. We are asking for the limpid pool, the clear blue sky. It stands to reason that we can't create either if we come to the horse with any predatory aggression, indecision, or inattention. Those attitudes just muddy the water.

To make things even more daunting, "level-headed" in humans means more than just becoming calm and receptive. It's not just a state we acquire and remain at. Level is also a verb—an action. It means we have to remain steady and composed no matter what is happening in the environment around us. It's easy to be serene when you're sitting on the mountaintop, but when things are getting a little bumpy between you and the horse—or between you and your kids, or you and your employees—it gets a little more challenging. And things are inevitably going to get bumpy no matter how obliging the horse. We have to learn to remain calm and level in the middle of stress, because nothing will cause a horse's head to go up faster than another creature—namely, you—out of alignment. We have to remain observant and tuned in to the horse and not give way to our frustrations. We can't allow ourselves to do what I did with Stella and make the horse the problem. We have to remain able to stay tuned in to the horse, take in information, and clearly assess what's causing the problems and what the horse needs from us. We have to remain aware, poised, and ready.

I thought a lot about level after my run-in with Stella. And the more I thought about that afternoon, the more I realized how level has come back again and again as a challenge in my own life, never more so than in the final breakdown of my marriage to Anita. The boundaries I set for myself, the self-discipline I lived by, wasn't working any more. My attitude when at work with the horses was getting worse, and a couple of times I caught myself precariously on the edge of losing my temper when things weren't going the way I wanted them to. It didn't happen often, but when it did it rattled me deeply. It was the opposite of everything I was trying to achieve, yet there I was letting myself get out of hand, making the horse the problem when I was the one who was full of frustration and anger. There were times I was pacing the cage with so much of both I hardly recognized myself. I once punched my fist through one of the walls of our home and barely even noticed what I was doing. Slowly, I began to understand that self-discipline wasn't going to be enough, that no matter how strictly I policed the boundaries I'd set for myself, something inside was out of balance.

I had never wavered in following my vision. Even before I met Anita, I had dreamed of a place where I could share what I'd learned with other like-minded riders and kindred spirits, a place where I could also be with my family and not have to travel so much. I guess I was looking for a home where my body, mind, and spirit could find both peace and fulfillment. Gradually, however, Anita had ceased to share that dream as she came to realize it was my vision and not hers. We both knew it but never faced up to it. And that unspoken conflict came to infect everything we did together. I sometimes felt as if Anita were trying to sabotage my efforts and undercut my determination, but she was just trying to find her own way, and, like a horse, she was finding out where to go by knowing where not to go. It was beginning to become clear that where I wanted and needed to go was not her direction in life, and as we tried to stay on a path that was obviously diverging, it took less and less for the ugly head of my anger to rear up.

When we first got married, Anita and I thought we both wanted the same things. However, as the first few years went by and Anita found herself putting her career with the horses (as an aspiring show jumper) on hold to be a stay-at-home-mom for our kids, she was finding that she had less and less desire to return to the show ring. She had been riding competitively since she was a child and by her early thirties she was beginning to realize that she had other interests that she wanted to explore outside the world of horses. Fair enough, but she was also feeling the call to move from our ranch in the country into town so that she could have "a real life" with friends and neighbors. I couldn't blame her; after all, I'd be gone for two or three weeks at a time, out on the road doing my job, while she'd be at home alone with our kids and the dogs and horses, the only adult around for miles as she coped with life as a single mom in our little house on the prairie. She wanted a new life in town, and a new career where she could aspire to become more than just "Chris Irwin's wife," and as soon as Adler was old enough to start school she was determined to do just that. Meanwhile, with all the traveling I was doing I felt more compelled than ever to stay true to my dream of finding and developing a wilderness equestrian retreat.

As the honeymoon wore off and the years of marriage began to catch up with us, the differences in our lifestyle choices began to tear us apart. She liked collecting exotic pets, especially birds, lots of them, but when I was home, exhausted from my work out on the road, I couldn't stand the noise of all those birds and it broke my heart and angered me to see so many winged creatures living locked up in cages. My disdain and anger toward her hobby certainly didn't help calm the waters. Then, although we tried our best to avoid conflict with each other, the stress would suddenly flare up again whenever I felt that she tended to cave in and spoil the children when they got too demanding. Of course, as you might expect, when it came to the kids she most often felt that I was far too serious and too strict with them. We each had our own ideas about priorities for the family, what was in the best interests of our children, and how our disposable income should be spent. We had started out on a journey together, with what we thought was a shared vision, but when we came to the inevitable forks in the road that test every marriage, we could seldom agree on which direction to take. I felt that she was beginning to resent the demands of my career, and I was beginning to resent her resentment.

When we finally did split up, the sudden release of tension was like a gust of cool, fresh air entering a stuffy room. It cleared my head, and I could think at last about what had gone wrong. As I traveled in solitude from clinic to clinic, stable to stable, talking with my students about the concepts I'm outlining in this book, I realized I had gotten one of the fundamentals wrong myself. Simply put, I had been out of alignment. Anita and I were like two front wheels on a car, one veering to the right and one angled left. The friction was burning us out, and everything I was trying to drag along with us, our kids and our business, was shuddering with the vibration as I tried to drive our family down the road. My own inner sense of level and balance was becoming as wobbly as an old wagon wheel full of broken spokes.

ROBIN CHAPIN

Nevada, early 1990s. Chris stays calm, aware, and focused as he works with a strong team of "runaway" Percheron draft horses. The team had been handled by a driver who pulled the reins to steer them, causing them to work with inverted spines while hitched incorrectly and dangerously to a wagon. When the adrenaline and fear finally became too much for the horses, they tried to run away from the wagon they were hitched to. When the desperate team of horses inevitably crashed the wagon into the trees, the wreck resulted in the driver being hospitalized and the team being sent to Chris for retraining. Here Chris is just beginning to drive the team "in hand," without pulling and with diagonal flexing exercises that soon brought the team to level-headed and calm.

I began to realize that there are as many ways to be knocked off our level perch as there are horses to knock us off. Their stubbornness can prick our pride, leading us to make bad decisions. Let's not forget about Stella and me. Horses' aggression can frighten us into responding with our own. They can fool us by manipulating our desire to bond with them, pretending to submit while still sticking out a defiant hip or constantly shoving their head into our space. These are all susceptibilities we bring into the round pen with us. If we have them (and we all do), the horses will root them out and they will use them against us. Remember, they are constantly challenging our fitness to lead. They have to know where we're weak, because we are the ones trying to convince them we're reliable enough to keep them safe.

So before we're able to lead our horses confidently into anything approaching level, we have to find it ourselves. That doesn't necessarily mean we must fix all our flaws before we enter the barn. It would be great if you could, but you'd probably be the first. The best the rest of us can hope for is to be aware of our triggers. If we know we frustrate easily, we must be willing to work on patience while we identify what types of situations aggravate us the most. If we anger quickly, we must learn not to let it blind us and learn to recognize which challenges set us off in the first place. If we are martyrs who are quick to rescue and enable victims to stay stuck in their own ruts, then we must learn the value of tough love. If we are easily distracted we must learn to focus. If we can focus but not keep track of the big picture, then we need to take off the blinders and develop more awareness. If we are timid we must learn to stand our ground. We must be willing to dig deep, develop confidence, and display assertive but nonthreatening authority with our body language. If we are intense and driven, the proverbial type A, our horses will need us to learn to lighten up so that we can push with the absolute least amount of pressure required.

In some ways, we learn to be level-headed the same way our horses learn focus—by learning where not to go. In other words, by building boundaries. Learning to be level-headed is a process of learning to recognize the triggers that cause us to bring about our own self-sabotage. Level-headed is, in many ways, the simple absence of all other dysfunctions.

Ultimately, whether we talk about level in horses or in humans, it comes down to the same thing. It's about being solidly centered and balanced. It's about not being easily rattled or distracted. It's about being focused, calm, composed, and responsive. But because we're the leader here, humans have a little extra responsibility. We have to develop the extra self-awareness that allows us to understand when we're losing our level. We have to figure out what circumstances become catalysts for the emotional reactions that cause us, to use another old horse cliché, to rear our ugly heads. A lot of riders—and people in general—live in denial about those catalysts. It's always someone else's fault, or the fault of bad equipment, or—least likely of all—the fault of the horse. This won't wash with our horses or anywhere else, really. If we are serious about wanting to be the boss, we have to take responsibility when things go wrong and try to understand what our role was in creating the problem. And we have to be able to do this under stress, in the middle of an environment when things are falling apart all around us. If Ernest Hemingway was right about courage being grace under pressure, then level is a type of courage.

Getting level right is a necessary step to any sort of lasting achievement with your horse. Because it works on the rider as deeply as it works on the mount, level is the open door to the bond we're looking for between human and animal. Let's return to all those racetrack clichés with which I opened this chapter. In a race that's neck-and-neck, that's going down to the wire, which horse is going to have the fastest gallop down the home stretch? It'll be the one who is completely focused on the finish, leaving all the posturing of the pack behind, straining toward the tape. It'll be the horse who is level-headed.

But even though I finally figured out what had been happening to me during the final years with Anita, my own struggle with level was far from over. Anita and I agreeing to disagree and head off in different directions didn't solve all my problems, and in fact created some new ones—chief among them, how to remain a father to my children. I refused to be the kind of parent that I had suffered with, and I was never cruel or abusive to my kids. My kids genuinely love their dad and I love them so much it often hurts unbearably that my work takes me so far away for such long periods of time. In many ways, my kids also bring out the very best in my behavior. But not being a bad dad wasn't exactly my idea of being a good father and I wasn't sure where and how my future with Raven and Adler lay. But at least now I wasn't trying to drag Anita along into a future and lifestyle she wanted no part of. At least now, my own path was clear. As I thought about it, I applied the lessons I was giving my students to my own life. I realized that I was now circling back, trying to correct mistakes I'd made that were preventing both Anita and me from moving forward. Getting out of an alignment that had gone bad wasn't in itself going to end my problems with level. I still had a ways to go, but at least now, I realized, I was beginning to bow more and rear my ugly head less.

[8]

ride by the
seat of your pants

I'M A LUCKY guy in almost too many ways to count. Despite the difficulties and moments of darkness I've shared in this book, I feel for the most part that I have been very fortunate in life. With all the blessings I've been given it was natural for me to feel that even though my marriage wasn't working out I still had lots going for me and lots to look forward to. After months and months of the two of us talking things over, I finally moved out of the house I shared with Anita and into my motor home in the fall of 2000. At the age of forty-one, as I resumed the life of a gypsy after my third "failed" marriage, I had no great hopes or expectations that I would ever find my "true love." A soul mate just did not appear to be in my cards, and with all I had going for me I was ready to accept my fate willingly. Sure enough, not unlike needing to give up control to gain control, as soon as I stopped trying to find true love, true love found me.

I had received an invitation to do a five-day clinic at a guest ranch in Steamboat Springs, Colorado. The day I got there, I was passing through the lobby after checking in and noticed a tall, slim woman with long brown hair having a conversation with the desk clerk. It was clear the woman wasn't happy about something, but she wasn't giving anyone a hard time. She was lighthearted and forceful at the same time. I was intrigued.

The next morning, I found myself sitting at the only available seat in the dining hall, across from the brown-haired woman at breakfast. She was in the middle of a conversation with a woman next to her about Friesians, praising the breed with passionate enthusiasm. I must have felt like causing a little mischief because my coyote nature came to life and I chimed in: "Excuse me, but I beg to differ. I've worked with a lot of Friesians and they're not all gentle giants. Just like any horse, they can come with problems, and when they do, they're typically larger than life." The brown-haired woman— who I couldn't help but notice, now that I was close to her, was very attractive—took up the challenge and gave me a feisty argument. That is, until the owner of the ranch stood up and introduced me to the group as their guest clinician. At that point she nodded to me with a little mocking deference and her green eyes filled with mischief. She was glowing with a presence that has long since become dulled in most people. She had a mystique I usually only see in animals. I was spellbound.

At the end of the meal, as people were rising to head outside to begin our day with the horses, I turned to her and said, "You know, I bet 98 percent of the men you meet turn tail and run the other way within minutes of saying hello." She grinned and said, "So why are you still standing here?" I grinned back at her. I liked this woman. She had spunk to burn. And I chuckled as I said, "Well, when you're used to dealing with twelve-hundred-pound horses, a little girl like you isn't going to scare me all that easy." After that, it was—as a horse might say—game on.

Her name was Kathryn Kincannon, and for the rest of that week, we seemed to be running into each other constantly. From our sessions with the horses it was clear that she was a natural athlete who had a rare level of awareness for her body. She was also an accomplished skier and devotee of tai chi and she had been riding on and off for years.

Needless to say she excelled at everything I showed her with the horses. She had other depths, too. One evening, I heard someone playing the saddest, yet most beautiful piano music I'd ever heard. I followed the sound into the music room and found Kathryn sitting at the keyboard, her eyes closed as she swayed with the music, entranced by her own haunting sound of unrequited love. When she finished she turned and faced me and we both had tears in our eyes. Neither of us said a word but we both knew what the other was feeling.

A barn dance had been scheduled for the last night of the clinic. There we sat at the same table, not quite sure of what was happening between us but sure that something was. We danced a few times and then the band took a break. We stepped outside for some fresh air, we kissed, and we weren't unsure anymore. Kathryn and I are now married. You could be forgiven for doubting the avowals of a man on his fourth wife, but there's no doubt in my heart. We two are perfectly aligned.

Kathryn is now the managing partner of our business and we travel together to the various events and clinics I give, where she's also become an invaluable assistant trainer and teacher. Sometimes these clinics are held in conjunction with competitive events. Although I used to compete enthusiastically at equestrian events—back in the early '90s I trained a few wild mustangs and their owners to numerous U.S. national championships in riding and driving events—I'm not really part of the competitive horse scene anymore. Occasionally, I have the good fortune to work with many top-notch athletes, both human and equine, who compete at all levels in western, English, jumping, driving, and endurance racing. But these days, when the competition actually begins I'm usually off at another clinic in another town getting back in the trenches and back to the basics. Still, my world intersects with the equestrian circuit with some regularity and one of the more exciting and spectacular places it happens is Spruce Meadows.

Spruce Meadows is a world-class equestrian facility just outside of Calgary, in the Canadian province of Alberta. It's rated the best show-jumping venue in the world. Although the focus at Spruce Meadows is primarily on the elite sport of world-class jumping, horses and riders from around the world meet there in the foothills just east of the Rocky Mountains every year to test each other in many different equestrian events, including the wildly popular "battle of the breeds" during "The Masters" in September. The competitors here are among the best in the world.

For me, watching the interaction between horse and rider is at least as interesting as the actual competition. That's what I was doing one morning at Spruce Meadows, standing outside a ring in which a number of riders and their mounts were warming up, happily passing the time before I did a short presentation on being the better horse. There were probably a dozen horses and riders at work, but a young German rider was the one who caught my eye. Part of her warm-up routine involved keeping her horse "on the rail" as she rode counterclockwise along the rail or perimeter fence of the arena. Every time, at a certain point by the in-gate where a group of onlookers was noisily hanging around, all of the horses would spook and move sideways off the rail through the boundary of the riders left (inside) leg and sideways away from the commotion. Now, the ring was a busy place that morning and there were any number of distractions that weren't going to be around come show time. My experience has been that most riders would have either simply ignored the horse's little quirk or would have madly spurred or used the whip to the body as it moved off the rail, trying to force the horse to bend back into the rail to teach the horse to respect the leg. The German rider, however, did something quite different.

While she still had her horse supple and straight on the rail, before she got to the problem at the gate, she set it up so that she was still on the rail but was now bending the horse off of the rail with her right leg instead of into the rail from her left. This is called counterbending. Anyway, sure enough, just like the rest of them, this horse started to shy off the rail. What was different was that her rider had proactively created the counterbend required to move off the rail in a balanced manner and she actually told the horse to side-pass in the very direction she was about to spook into. The rider was saying, in effect, "If you're going to move away from the gate to the left, this is how I want you to do it." Instead of working against the barrel of her horse with her left spur, she used her right leg to aid the horse in the direction she wanted to go. It was beautiful to watch—instead of it being a scared leap away from the crowd, the rider transformed it into a beautiful, flowing, perfectly aligned and balanced side-pass. After a few strides of the side-pass she simply turned the side-passing bend back to the rail. Without a suggestion of a fight, that rider both reinforced her control over her horse and allowed her to maintain the flow of her gait. She also earned a great deal of trust from that horse, because in the mind of a horse, its leader *should* push it away from scary places, not into them. That rider knew that a horse goes best into scary places when they're simply not all that scary anymore. As the other riders tried to force their horses "off" their left leg by spurring or whipping, they only confirmed for their horses that this was indeed a bad place in the arena. The problem only got worse instead of better as the horses lost all trust in the riders' ability to navigate through this scary place. As for the riders who ignored the spooky shy sideways away from the gate, their horses had little or no confidence or respect for their boundaries and those horses went on to be the ones who refused the more difficult jumps and ran away from the fences. However, the German rider who proactively set up the counterbend in order to push her horse away from the scary spot in the arena with a perfectly aligned and balanced leg yield increased both the respect and trust of her horse while building confidence and keeping the situation calm. After a few times around the arena repeating the same exercise, her horse found out that the gate wasn't such a bad place after all and soon lost all inhibition about going by the gate. Suspicion quickly became confidence and curiosity. Within a few more laps, the need for the counterbending leg yield away from the gate was finished, as the horse was no longer leery of the area. The

German gal was the only rider in the arena who could keep her horse on track and on the rail by the gate. That rider's skill and insight impressed me, and it must have impressed her horse as well, because the two of them went out to easily win their very difficult class, the only ones in their division to go a clear round without knocking down a single fence rail.

That split second along the rail was a tiny moment. I'm sure no one else marked it and the rider herself probably thought nothing of it as soon as it was over. But what she achieved with that elegant little side-pass is the subject of this entire chapter. The word "bend" has come up many times already. It's so integral to my kind of horse sense that you can't really talk about anything without the subject coming up. But now it's time to look at bend in a bit more depth.

"Bend," to me, is about one thing: adaptability. It's not so much about creating a turn by flexing the horse's barrel. The horse is going to do that anyway. The kind of understanding of bend that I like to see, the kind that the young German rider demonstrated so casually and expertly at Spruce Meadows, is the kind that creates direction using the horse's natural motion and movement. It's about using what the horse gives us, allowing us to advance one step further in our mutual relationship without endangering our level-headedness, our timing, our contact or our clean, smooth forward. Like the German jumper at Spruce Meadows, it's about giving up control to gain control.

The proper use of bend depends on a proper understanding of how a horse moves. We've already touched on this: horses move forward through a series of related diagonals. Weight moves from right rear to left front and left rear to right front. Horses are not like conveyor belts. They're more like skaters. For the rider, this means that a horse's forward progress is actually slightly serpentine, like a skier cutting tight S-turns down the fall line. It follows, then, that the horse's spine is almost always slightly bent one way or the other. I'll repeat that, because I see very few riders who seem to understand it: the horse's spine bends with every single stride, whether we're in a turn or not.

As we've already discussed, this has profound implications for how we time our requests. But this fact of horse physiology should also shape so much more.

The first issue riders have to come to grips with when they start dealing with bend is their own physical inhibitions. We've already mentioned that because of the horse's gait, we have to ride with a little swing. And where does swing come from? The hips.

If there is one part of the body that North American society seems to have been specifically designed to lock up, it's the hips. Remember the furor over Elvis? They weren't even allowed to show his hips on TV at first. Why? Because the hips are the seat of sexuality and sexuality makes us, as a culture, clamp down like a chastity belt. We live in a culture suffused with sexual messages in everything from TV ads to movies, but when it comes to our own warm and breathing bodies, well, we'd rather change the subject. The hips open a Pandora's box of scary, uncontrollable forces that we'd prefer not to confront, at least not in polite society. As a riding instructor, I can actually see people stiffen up at the mere mention of their hips. They practically stop breathing when I ask them if I can take hold of their hips to show them something. Most of my students freeze up a little when I talk about their hips. Then they're self-conscious about them, which also causes problems. People lock up and brace their hips the way inverted horses lock up and brace their backs. And there are few things about a rider a horse will notice sooner than a locked-up, got-no-rhythm seat. That rider won't even get good quality forward, let alone the subtleties of bend.

Men are the worst—not that it's entirely their fault. "White men can't dance" is one of the few ethnic comments we're still allowed to make in polite society, and rare is the man brave enough to be the first on the dance floor. Not only might he have to move his hips, but—horrors!—everyone will be watching. In our culture, men are alienated from their bodies unless they're using them to catch a football or chase a puck. Anything to do with sexual display is reserved for women. It's somehow manlier to sit back and watch. It doesn't make sense, really. A man who dances, just like a man who cooks (or rides horses), won't lack for female company—which, after all, is generally considered desirable. But go to a nightclub or a wedding and it's all the same. There are as many women dancing together as there are male-female pairs.

There is help. Dance classes aren't a bad idea, but if you're not ready for that, exercise systems such as yoga, tai chi, and Pilates all focus on flowing, graceful movement, core strength, and a greater connection between mind and body. And maybe it wouldn't hurt to play a little hip-shaking funk or some sultry Brazilian samba around the house now and then. At least learn to recognize that if you're having trouble finding a good seat in your saddle, it's probably not because of the horse. Duke Ellington was right: it don't mean a thing if it ain't got that swing. Free your hips and your mind will follow.

A loose, supple midsection is a crucial introduction to the concept of bend because it allows you to feel the rhythm of the horse's gait. It's silly really, how many people are out there trying to feel their horse's feet, as if it's some kind of psychic phenomenon to be able to sense the rhythm of your horse's footfall. The problem is that you can't make yourself feel the movement of your horse's legs in your mind—you need to feel it in the seat of your pants. Think of it this way: when we ride we are not sitting on the legs, we are sitting on the barrel. What connects the back legs to the front legs is the barrel, so we feel the legs of the horse through the swinging of the barrel and we interpret the swinging of the barrel as we feel it through the receptivity of our hips. Therefore, the only way to know when and where your horse's feet are is to be able to feel the rhythm of your own hips. If you can combine the intellectual or theoretical understanding of what's happening in your horse's spine with the feel of the physical groove of how it plays out, you can start manipulating the bend and the horse will keep on dancing right with you.

I see a lot of riders who get stuck here. They know about bend and they sit on the horse as if they were joined to it, but they don't take the next step. They try to force their own bend on the horse rather than work with what the horse is giving them. They're taught—and this is very common—that the horse must be made to respect the rider's leg. This is not quite true. It's much better to say the horse must want to respect the rider's leg, but too often that crucial distinction is not made. The problem is that the phrase "made to respect" seems to give the rider permission to impose his will over how the horse bends. Horses, however, don't like having their bend controlled. Bend is fundamental to their sense of balance and surrendering control of that crucial function creates stress. That stress is likely to cause the horse to resist and invert its spine, fill its head with adrenaline, and fall off track. And for a "made to respect" rider, that means it's time to bring out the whip and spurs.

For a good, consistent rider, this can get results—of a kind. Almost all but the most intensely competitive horse can be forced to respect the horse games of who pushes whom, even when they're being played by a bully. However, the result is often a sullen horse. In addition, the "made to respect" approach doesn't deal with the issue of why the horse resisted the bend in the first place. That resistance isn't going to go away, and the desired bend is going to get harder and harder to achieve. Sooner or later, the frustrated rider is going to start pulling on the horse's face on the inside rein to create the bend that should be happening in the barrel from the inside seat bone and leg. Pulling on the rein does nothing to arc the body into a balanced bend. But if you start the bend with your leg on the barrel, the neck flexes naturally into the turn. This is a huge problem in both English and western barns where trainers and coaches are pulling horses for flexion instead of bending them. No horse likes to be pulled and all horses move better and more freely with the balance that can be found in bending from the leg. What gets me is not the riders who do not know better, but the vast majority of trainers and coaches in English barns all over North America who talk the talk of bending from the inside leg but keep coaching their students to "tip" or "initiate" the nose of the horse into the turn with the inside rein. Call it tip, initiate, guide, or whatever you want, but pulling the inside rein on a horse is fundamentally backward and totally counterintuitive to the horse. As I asked earlier, when was the last time you saw a horse grab hold of another horse by the mouth and drag it around?

Chris creates a turn by bending the skis from the core of his body.

KATHRYN KINCANNON-IRWIN

Here's another way to think about correct bend. Skiers turn their skis by bending them from their midsection into an arc. How much bend do you think even the best skier could get if he tried to turn his skis by pulling on two ropes attached to his ski tips?

The best way to get bend in your horse—and the only way that will keep her convinced you're on her side—is to be willing to start out at work with the bend that's already happening in the natural motion of her gait. The trick is to tune in to that and convince your horse that you don't want to control the bend, simply adapt it and improve it. You're saying, "I know how important it is to you to be able to bend your body however you need to. I'm not trying to take that away from you. In fact, if you follow me I'll show you a way to accentuate your bend so it is better and smoother. I can shape it better than you can, for I am the better horse."

And they will allow us to do this. Why? Remember the physiological benefits of smooth, balanced motion in a horse: a level head that's full of happy chemicals. Horses experience this in the wild, but never for very long, and if we can create that relaxed sense of well-being in them for extended periods our horses are never going to want us to dismount. This is what I mean by giving up control to get it. When we improve upon the bend the horse is doing naturally, we actually get better control than if we insisted on forcing her body into a bend of our devising.

$\mathcal{I}$T HELPS SOMETIMES to stand back and think about the big picture: nature seldom expresses itself with straight lines. Practically everything in nature is curved, from the bank of a river to the petal of a flower to the vast spirals and arcs of weather systems. Even your own DNA is made of interwoven bending spirals. Prey consciousness is also much more attuned to curves. As opposed to our straight-ahead goal-oriented predator mindset, horse awareness is much more like ripples spreading out in a pond. It's even best to approach a horse walking in an arc. As a general rule, I find things go much smoother if we work with natural laws instead of against them. Your horse's instinctive bend is just one more curve in a universe full of them. Go with it.

Leadership is another important issue that comes into play with bend. This is, and has always been, about leadership. We want the horse to surrender control of its bend because we want to lead it somewhere. Leadership, however, means more than just acknowledging the horse's bend and working with it. We also have to use bend to help us earn the horse's trust.

I'll give an example, something I see on a weekly basis in riding arenas all over North America. One of the most common problems riders have with their horses is getting them to go into corners. If you can look at the situation with prey consciousness, it's not hard to understand why this situation is so tense. The horse looks at a corner—any corner, even if it's just a right angle formed by two fence rails—and gets claustrophobic. Suddenly, two of the four directions are blocked off. The horse's possible escape routes are reduced by half. Simply put, horses don't like going into corners because they smell a trap.

Still, the riders don't understand that. Or if they do understand that, they don't care or they don't know what to do about it. They only know that the horse must respect their inside leg, so they keep using it to put pressure on their horses to keep them heading into the corners, which the horses fight against. So it becomes a big struggle. That calm, focused awareness on which everything depends quickly deteriorates. And the riders come to me and say their horses have behavior problems.

Here, we have to return to first principles. Everything we're trying to do with the horse we're trying to achieve on a basis of mutual respect and trust. Everything we do should increase the faith our horses place in us. Look at the problem from the horse's perspective. Would you trust a leader who was trying to force you to go first into a possible trap? Probably not. And here comes the refrain: Anything we want to create in the horse we must first create in ourselves, and that applies to physical situations, too. If we want the horse to be willing to go into what looks like it might be a trap, we have to demonstrate that we're willing to go in first.

That doesn't mean that we need to dismount and walk our horses into corners from the ground or get off to lead them into a river or over a bridge so that we can always go first. What that means is that when the horse starts to bend away from the corner, don't vise-grip it with your legs in order to deny that bend. Let it bend. If you have been riding at "trot rising," you must now post on the other diagonal because a horse bent correctly needs the rider to post up and down with the correct "outside" shoulder diagonal. However, a horse that has pushed through the rider's inside leg and is now bent "incorrectly" will need the rider to ride the "incorrect" diagonal in order to keep the horse balanced. I know this sounds confusing, but far too many so called "educated" riders have been taught to "rise and fall with the leg against the wall" and they assume that because they are trotting to the left they should be posting up and down with the right shoulder, and vice versa. As they trot right they assume to post up and down in time with the left shoulder. These people have been taught to ride the arena instead of their horses. The correct diagonal to post up and down with in order to help balance yourself and your horse at the trot has nothing to do with which direction you are riding in the arena and has everything to do with how your horse is bending.

If you can do this, you can go first into the corner for your horse without dismounting. You ride the counterbend away from the corner by making it your idea, but as you bend away you also block the horse from actually shying away (with what was the inside leg but is now the outside leg). Then, for those few strides through the corner, your body and your push will be between the horse and the scary corner. It will only be for a few strides but that's enough for the horse. She'll see that the corner holds no terrors for her leader, who is perfectly willing to face it. At this point, usually sooner rather than later, the corner's threat will fade. The horse will most likely even become curious about it and will head into it eagerly. Instead of fomenting a battle, which creates resentment that will likely sabotage you later on, you've used bend to remove a source of tension for the horse. She will be relieved, and you will be the object of her gratitude. And once a horse is calm and confident about her rider, then and only then will she allow him to easily control her barrel.

JINX FOX

While in Nevada, Chris gentled and trained Miwok, a wild mustang, for work in harness and coached her owner, Karen Malloy, on how to drive. Together they went on to win 10 U.S. national championships in driving events.

(I need to be clear about this. I am not talking about always enabling horses who push through the inside leg. What I'm saying is that if we know how to ride a counterbending horse, on a counter diagonal, purposefully bending and leg-yielding away from fear instead of into it, within a few minutes you can bend into and leg-yield into the same scary place. The fear will have melted away and turned into calm, confidence, increased respect, trust, and curiosity. This is a temporary or transitional exercise in working with the body, mind, and spirit of the horse in order to earn enough emotional authority so that it is realistic to ask the horse to give us control of its barrel.)

This is the understanding that the young German rider at Spruce Meadows demonstrated. I don't see that kind of understanding very often and when I do, more often than not it's from a European rider. I'm not going to win very many friends for myself by saying this, but the horse culture in Europe has a much more sophisticated sense of bend than we do on this continent. We pat ourselves on the back a lot and tell ourselves and anyone who'll listen about how important the horse has been in North American history and how the horse is part of our culture and in our blood, but I believe the facts tell a slightly different story. When it comes to high-end, highly technical equestrian events such as jumping or dressage, Europeans come out ahead more often than not.

Between 1979 and 2004, thirteen European riders won World Cup jumping championships. Only ten North Americans have—and none of those have occurred since 1989, the glory days of Canada's Big Ben and Ian Millar. Before the 2004 Athens Olympics, only one North American woman was in the top five world dressage rankings. Yes, those Olympics saw the American team win five medals, more than any other country. But none of them were gold. And despite the fact that David O'Conner won gold for the USA in three-day eventing at the previous Olympics, the three top-ranked equestrian nations coming out of the Athens games were Germany, Great Britain, and France.

And Canada? We like to cry that it's all about money and that our poor showing on the world stage is because we can't compete with the war chests of Americans and Europeans. But that's not what the Europeans say. The Europeans will tell us over and over again that the biggest difference between the continents is that young European riders are taught how to ride correctly on very well-trained horses whereas very few North Americans ever know what it's like to feel a perfectly balanced horse underneath them. As well, the Europeans start their young horses out correctly so students learn right from the start how things should feel. Like children, how these horses perform in high school depends upon how they did in grade school, and our horses and trainers are most often failing as far back as kindergarten. No amount of spurring, whipping, or money will develop a soft, supple horse that is ready, willing, and able to bend around the merest suggestion from a rider's inside seat bone or leg. Only learning to think horse, speak horse, and ride with the mind of a leader in the herd will.

I know there are top-flight riders in many countries. And I've already acknowledged that I'm not really a member of that part of the equestrian world. But I go to more than a few competitions and I see a lot of horse people from all over. I even work with many of the riders who compete at those events, so I believe I'm qualified to make the judgment I've made. Far too many North Americans tend to force the bend like bullies; Europeans work with it like ballet. I don't know if it's because the days when cowboys helped "win the West" are a lot closer in North America, but there is a lingering buckaroo flavor to our horse culture and that arrogance doesn't always serve us well. We've got a lot to learn from across the Atlantic.

I hope we learn those lessons soon, because this understanding of bend opens up many more gates than just the ones in your horse's mind. Just as we adapt to the bend of our horse, we must adapt to the curves life sends us as well.

I'll give you an example. For the first year and a half after Kathryn and I met, we maintained a long-distance relationship. She'd join me on the road when she could and when I could I'd visit her where she lived in Lake Placid, New York. I noticed that when Kathryn and I were at her place she was much more tense and stressed than when she was on the road with me. Of course, it was because of her job. Kathryn managed a very high-end luxury resort hotel, and although she was very fond of the founding partners, there were a couple of executives above her in the corporate food chain who were relentless in their demands and stingy in their praise. One night I was waiting for her at her house, dinner ready, candles lit, and in the door came a very unhappy Kat. She was mad and hurt and didn't know whether to kick something or just cry. I massaged her feet and poured her a glass of wine. And then she cried and told me about her day.

Earlier that day, her corporate masters had held a meeting to go over the month-end financials. Kathryn was looking forward to it. She had more than met their goals on many fronts and was especially proud of the profit on room revenues. Budgeted at 65 percent, the hotel had reached an astounding 72 percent! She was expecting and deserved congratulations and high praise for this. At least a big pat on the back, if not a celebratory bottle of champagne. Instead, when they got to her report on room revenues, one of the type A executives looked at her straight-faced and said: "So—72 percent. What's it going to take to make 80 percent?" At that point Kathryn was crushed and disgusted. She felt like walking out of that room and quitting.

Again, lucky me. I saw my opening and took it. I asked Kathryn to give her notice and come work with me. At first she laughed and said, "you can't afford me." I told her she was right, at least for now. But then I added that with her management skills the business would grow to be more than big enough for both of us within just a few months. It didn't take Kathryn very long to make the leap, and she gave her notice, sold her house, and took the chance of coming to work with me. She's nothing if not adaptable, and with her at my side I've been able to do things I could only dream about when I was on my own.

Ultimately, what I'm saying is that it's much more productive to work with circumstances than against them—"circumstances" being understood in the broadest possible sense. It could mean anything from the strengths and weaknesses of your spouse to the characteristics and abilities of a coworker. It can also mean we should play to our own strengths and stop trying to be something we're not or something we feel we should be. Life goes a lot smoother and easier if we learn to open our eyes and simply be aware of what is and stop acting on our idea of what should be. If we stop trying to force our will on the world and instead try to work with what we're given, we'll be much, much better off. Video gamers learn to look for little secrets that programmers have hidden within the game that let them ascend to the next level or defeat a particularly nasty opponent. We have to adopt the same approach to the world: What's already out there that I can use? Who can I bring on to my side, and what can I do to convince that person to make common cause with me? It's about wanting what you truly need instead of needing what you want. As Mick Jagger and the Rolling Stones said "You can't always get what you want, but if you try some time, you just might find, you get what you need."

That approach encourages us to look around, to notice things, to pay attention to people. It requires us to be aware, instead of simply forging ahead. It teaches us to see potential allies instead of obstacles. It needs us to be subtle and supple, instead of blunt and unyielding. It opens up our focus, instead of narrowing our vision to exclude everything but our immediate aims. It creates a sense of group and team accomplishment, instead of glorifying a single mighty visionary.

Sound familiar? It should. If you were thinking "sounds like horse sense," you're catching on.

[9]

raising the bar

I'VE WRITTEN ELSEWHERE how important music was to me when I was growing up. It gave me both emotional release and some much-needed pats on the back from the people around me, especially from those of my friends who also played. Music was my first sanctuary in a disappointing and often crazy-scary world. It took a while, however, before I was good enough to earn any applause. It took loads of patience and dedication to learn my scales and my chords before I could make anything like music.

For the last six chapters, we've also been talking about scales and chords. We've laid out the fundamentals, the do-re-mi of the equine symphony. This chapter will be the last in that series, the seventh note in the scale. We're finished tuning up. Now, we're about to jam.

The last chapter left off at learning to give up control of the horse's bend in order to gain control of it. Through understanding that bend and working with it instead of against it, we've got our horse relaxed and happy, supple as a fish and willing to work. Through careful attention to all the other previous concepts—alignment, forward, contact, timing, and level—we've developed a horse who is calm and smooth, increasingly focused on us. I said in the second chapter that this whole

Chris playing guitar and singing at a wedding.

exercise was about control, about who was going to push whom. Well, now that we've got control, what are we going to do with it?

At this point, it's time to shift our intent. Until now, I've talked about the need for focus. Now, it's time to talk about maximizing potential. Until now, I've talked about the need for creating calm. Now, it's time to create energy. This is when we start to work on increasing the horse's athletic ability and our ability to make use of it. It's time to maximize some horse power.

Whenever we want to teach our horses something new, there's only one strategy. As always, we return to basic principles. There's really only one way horses learn anything. We push them forward. But this time, we push them forward into more boundaries. We are going to take that supple, focused, level-headed horse and push her through an increasingly intricate series of blocks and commands. As the horse's options for direction become narrower and narrower, we are going to concentrate her energy the way water speeds up as it runs through a funnel. At a certain point (and it's different for every horse), she will enter a new psychological state. When she does, like musicians you and your horse will be riffing and scatting in perfect harmony.

But first, a warning. I stress a lot of fundamental skills in my approach to horses. My students spend a lot of time on the ground working with the horses and we're constantly thinking about simple basics such as body language and consistent behavior. I emphasize that the only way to learn these essentials is by repetition and practice. I really work on conveying the understanding that just like learning the scales in music, there are certain approaches that must be

ANITA IRWIN

Chris' daughter Raven practicing the fundamentals or "scales" with Dad during a clinic in Mexico

so internalized that they become instinctive. I'm convinced that this is the way to go, but I'm aware that this approach does have pitfalls.

One pitfall—the main one that concerns us here—I call the Riding the Scales Syndrome. It almost always involves unusually conscientious students. They ride regularly. They never miss arena time. When they get a chance to work out with their horses, they're there. And they're very careful to get things right. You can almost hear the mental checklist as they follow the book step-by-step. And in order to get a step right, to play that scale perfectly, they do it over and over again. I once watched a dressage rider work her horse through the same twenty-meter circle at least forty-seven times. Forty-seven!

There's no way it should take a horse that long to learn something new. If it's taking forty-seven tries to get the response you want, chances are you've missed a step and something more fundamental needs fixing first. After about eight successful repetitions of something, the horse has got it pretty much figured out. After more than just a few repetitions of the same thing, she's starting to get bored. And you know what they say about an idle mind—well, it goes triple for equine minds. Like Dennis the Menace, a horse that's no longer needing to listen to her rider about where she's going has got nothing else to do but think up devilment about how to be contrary and challenge the rider. It's not really true that practice makes perfect. Repeating the same mistakes will only perfect your mistakes. I much prefer this version of that old saying: it takes perfect practice to make perfect.

Remember, the horse is a prey animal and, as such, is constantly concerned about everything, including the quality of her leadership. So once your commands are no longer challenging the horse, she's going to start challenging you. It's not because she's being bad. It's just that for her safety, she needs to know where your weaknesses are. It's like a group of political reporters during an election—they probe the candidates for weaknesses because voters have to be able to make informed decisions. The harder the reporters dig, the more fully informed the electorate and the more confident it is in casting its ballot (at least, that's the theory). You could say that the best and most challenging horses are like investigative reporters probing to find and reveal gaps in your integrity and credibility as their leader. Maybe I should call my next driving team "Woodward and Bernstein."

Just as a determined reporter won't quit until he's found his scoop, the horse won't quit until she's discovered something, either—a disrespectful bend she was allowed to get away with, a moment of inattention from the rider, poor timing of a cue, or the slightest gap in your boundaries. And every time she picks something up, a little static gets created in her mind and the smoothly flowing river the rider is trying to create gets a little choppier.

Here's a little anecdote to show just how hard a look the horse is going to give you. A little while ago, I had the chance to work with a rider on the short list for the Canadian national dressage team. She was, of course, an excellent rider, but she'd recently acquired a Dutch Warmblood that was giving her serious trouble. It was quite a horse— a quarter of a million dollars worth of bloodline and possibility—but it was also quite a hazard. One of two things would happen every time that rider showed up to ride: Her horse would either be a flawless dream come true or a nightmare that bolted or bucked her off at the mounting block.

I watched the woman ride and she was doing everything right. Her seat was plugged deeply into the saddle, she rode forward from back to front, proactive and wonderfully fluent in horse body language as it is spoken from the saddle. As long as she was in the saddle there was little or no problem. But when she was on the ground with her horse, it was only moments before the miscommunications started. While holding the horse, she'd turn to greet a friend and inadvertently aim her core into the horse's face—in horse, a provocation to battle and a leading cause of horse bites. Or she'd ignore a little bend into her while she was grooming. Or he'd lean into her with his shoulder, just a little as the two of them stood next to each other in the barn aisle, and she'd step out of his way, unconsciously allowing herself to be herded. It wasn't happening all the time, but it was happening enough. To her, the ride either had not begun, or was over, and when she wasn't in the tack the horse was no longer her prime focus. But to the horse, it was never over. As far as he was concerned, when they were together on the ground she was inconsistent and, like the vast majority of riders, passive-aggressive in her responses to his challenges. The horse was noticing this and the contradiction was confusing him. And when the rider decided enough was enough and administered a little correction, the perceived inconsistency really pissed him off.

It didn't take much to fix the problem. Elite dressage riders are famous for preaching "we need to ride our horses every step." I just told her that she needed to develop the same religious consistency with her dressage principles on the ground, in everything she did with her horse, as she had when she was in the saddle. As I showed her how to lunge her horse with her body to his body instead of his head, and I showed her how to lead him "in hand" with all the same principles of contact she applies with conviction from the saddle, the horse revealed his true potential and all his anger and frustration melted away within moments. Before long, the two were cleaning up and turning heads on the dressage circuit.

Look, I know I'm a hard case on consistency. It's the bedrock of everything I teach about horsemanship. And in fact, it's at the heart of my approach to life. Consistency equals integrity in my book. But we're all human and we're all going to make mistakes or overlook something. Lord knows I did with Stella. No rider is perfect. If, however, we give a bored horse forty-seven repetitions to just sit there underneath us and wait for us to stutter or mispronounce something in a body language most of us barely speak, we are setting ourselves up for trouble and failure again and again.

The answer, quite simply, is to mix it up and keep it interesting. A horse has at least four gaits if we include backing up, each with several different speeds. There are infinite variations and patterns on four directions and two ways to bend. We have to use them. Keep changing the bend. Sometimes, simply stop. Use your hands only to create boundaries of where not to go, never pulling on the face, steering from your core, making transitions timed perfectly with the diagonal balance and rhythm of the barrel. A horse listens best and stays tuned in when she knows that she will be given clear and consistent directions, but she has no idea what she will be asked to do or where she will be asked to go next. The horse is poised, not knowing what's next, but is ready, willing, and able to perform with power and grace. So keep filling the horse's brain with transitions. Repeat moves if there's resistance or if you didn't communicate something clearly, but don't get stuck in a rut. Remember the law of 1-2-3-4: when a horse gets something right once, that's a fluke; twice is coincidence; three times is a pattern; and four times means she's got it and can now predict what's going to come next. When she's got it, move on. Or as an old horseman I once knew used to say, when a horse gives you what you want, stop asking.

How many transitions are enough? Well, consider a dressage routine. A four-minute routine could easily contain forty different transitions. That's one every six seconds or so, probably a faster pace of change than your average figure skating routine. Now, you may not achieve that level anytime soon, and maybe never. The important thing is to start from wherever you are and get busy. Be patient and don't try to move ahead too quickly, but don't be satisfied with simply pacing back and forth through the scales.

So there are three factors we have to bring together. The first is a steady, consistent push forward for impulsion from the hindquarters of the horse. It's where everything starts and it's a crucial part of every single horse concept I teach. The second factor is firm and consistent but elastic boundaries from the seat, legs, and hands. The horse must be constantly stepping forward into boundaries that don't inhibit her forward movement or pull on her face, but simply channels her ener

ANITA IRWIN

Chris in Mexico working on transitions to develop collection with a young Hanoverian stallion.

gy by sealing off all directions except the one specific path we want the horse to follow with free-flowing impulsion. The third factor is a string of clear commands rapid enough to focus the horse's mind and encourage it to be respectful enough to keep it clear of static. At the right frequency of transitions, the horse will be more than just focused. She will be poised and light on her feet, ready for anything and completely attuned to what's next. She will say to herself, "I have no idea what we're going to do next, but I'd better be ready. I'd better start to collect myself."

We've talked before about collection. This, finally, is how it starts to actually happen. The horse's back legs are creating a lot of power in reaction to our push, but because we're bending the horse and channeling its movement, the horse can't simply churn it into forward and blast ahead. Some of that power has to be stored. What happens when you've got forward energy surging into rapidly shifting boundaries is that the rounded, cycling thrust from the horse's hindquarters flows through the spine and into the shoulders and the neck. The horse's spine starts to flex upward, storing power like a bow flexed by an arrow pointed at the sky. The horse's hindquarters actually drop a little as she lengthens her stride from behind, reaching farther forward underneath herself, and her back and neck lifts. It evolves into what's called an "uphill" horse. This is collection.

A collected horse is capable of amazing gymnastics. I'll give you an example. Imagine you're riding counterclockwise around the outside of the round pen (riding circles to the left) and with a little bit of a bend from your left inside leg you begin to leg yield or push your horse into an enlarging spiral away from the rail of the round pen. Now, align your seat bones and hips so that your belly button is always centered perfectly between the ears of your horse and your spinal column and her spine are always perfectly centered. Your right leg is now just slightly ahead of the girth or axis of the arc in her body. You can now plant your right leg where your hip has aligned it and use it as a boundary for the horse's right or outside shoulder. Don't use it to push. That's the job of your left leg. Just plant it there like a post, rooted all the way down your spinal column into your hips. Now, at the same time we need to create blocking boundaries with the reins. In this left bend, your right rein says, "No, we're not turning left with this bend, just hold the bend without turning left," while your left rein says, "Whatever you do, do not try to look or turn right during this left bend or we'll really lose our balance." Now, as you're moving forward with your left inside leg bending the barrel of the horse, your right leg blocking the outside shoulder of the horse from "drifting" too far off to the right from your left bend, and both of your reins simply holding that bend in place without letting the horse turn left or right, you can then shift your left "inside leg" back and apply a pushing pressure farther back on the barrel just in front of the hindquarters. Now, with perfect timing from your left leg that only pushes the side of the horse with the pulse of their natural diagonal rhythm, your left leg asks the left hip of the horse to swing a few strides "over and out" to the right.

Whew. It sounds complicated, and, truth be told, it is. This is advanced equitation that requires the ability to stay supple and composed while multitasking, but when we get this maneuver right it's a lot like when a skateboarder gets to the top of the half-pipe, pushes down on the front of his board and flips the back end around for a 180° degree half spin. If you've done it right, and your horse is uphill enough, the back end will spin out to the right just like a racecar driver steering through a curve using only the throttle. By scissoring your legs like this, you can spin a collected horse's front end around its rear and its rear around its front. You can twirl a horse like a baton; this is called either a turn on the forehand or a turn on the haunches. It's simple enough for a horse to do but it isn't an easy message for a rider to communicate. That's one of my favorite aphorisms about horses: They're simple but not easy.

It takes a while to get a horse to this point. It's astounding to watch, like poetry in motion. It can and should take years of disciplined training. Unfortunately, the kind of patience this requires is in short supply, and the horses suffer. Especially in the impatient, fast-food, and fast-buck culture of North America, people look for a quick fix. As in so many things, we look for an easy, technological solution to a problem that should be resolved through our own resources. This is when the big, leveraged bits and training gimmicks come out. They work to a degree, but it's not the same. The horse looks collected, but the rise in the horse's back is minimal, as it is created by the force and resistance coming from an extreme bit in hands that pull back or because of chronic and improper use of draw reins and martingales. Instead, that collection, that reserve of power and agility, should be coming from a horse who is ready, willing, and able to collect itself. In some circles this is the difference between what is called "classically" collected horses, who develop self-carriage through quality training, and "competitively" collected horses, who are strongly forced into a hand held "headset."

Remember, we should never get in the horse's face by pulling to control her, whether with the halter or the bit. When the horse collects herself, she does so because she wants to be able to respond better to your commands. Collection should be her idea.

COLLECTION IS THE result of transitions that communicate more boundaries of "where not to go," an ever-intensifying discipline that comes on top of a sound foundation built all the way from proper alignment on up. If that foundation really is solid, the flow of new boundaries you're pushing the horse through will channel her energy in a more focused and precise manner, intensifying it until a new level is achieved. Take the word horse out of that last sentence and that process would be familiar to a lot of humans, as well. It should almost go without saying, but I'll say it again anyway: What we wish to see in the horse we must first create in ourselves. As we push our horses to collect themselves, a similar process must be under way in our own hearts. In humans, however, we give it a different name. We call it self-discipline.

We're familiar with the idea that self-discipline is necessary to achieve goals. On the crudest and most obvious level, if you want to run marathons it's a good idea to quit smoking. But self-discipline goes a lot deeper than that. In many ways, it's about setting boundaries for ourselves, just as we set them for the horses.

Sometimes, this process is very conscious. A friend of mine is a reporter; now and then he covers hearings held by Canada's national parole board to determine whether a prisoner has earned the privilege of early release. At every hearing, the board members ask the prisoner if he's aware of what circumstances lead him to commit crimes. The circumstances could be physical—he's drunk, he's with a certain crowd of friends, he's in a certain part of town. They could be mental, perhaps loneliness, fear, or boredom. But before the board even considers release, the prisoner has to have a complete understanding of what his criminal triggers are.

But that's not enough. The prisoner has to describe to the board what he's going to do if confronted with one or more of his triggers. The plan has to be detailed and specific. If, for example, he's going to depend on a buddy to come and haul him out of a bad situation or talk him down from something, he has to know the phone number by heart, know what hours the buddy is likely to be there and have an alternate or two in case he's not. In short, the prisoner has to have a clear, precise knowledge of what boundaries he has to set for himself. He has to know what triggers are most likely to push him past those boundaries and he has to have a plan for defusing those triggers.

Not that riding a horse is the same as getting out of jail—although it can feel that liberating—but that's the kind of disciplined introspection and boundary setting we need to go through ourselves.

Learning self-discipline is difficult, but it doesn't have to be a grim, negative experience. It can be exhilarating and, paradoxically, even liberating. It feels good to shed our old, destructive habits that frustrate our efforts at self-improvement. It's not fun to be frustrated—once we learn not to let frustration get the better of us, we're that much happier.

And just as they do for the horse, boundaries channel our efforts. Discipline creates intensity. The light from the sun gives everything a broad, even illumination. But if we use a magnifying glass to channel even a tiny bit of that light, we can create a pinpoint of solar energy that can burn holes in wood. Few people live lives that are more disciplined and surrounded by boundaries than religious monks. Their every hour is circumscribed, sometimes down to their dress. But I would guess few people live lives with more spiritual intensity.

Think of a sonnet. Every line in this poetic form must have certain rhythm and a certain rhyme. There's no flexibility here. That's what a sonnet is and if it doesn't follow the rules it's not a sonnet. But for centuries, poets have written sonnets to express their deepest and most passionate thoughts and feelings. I think there's a reason for that. I think the rigid boundaries themselves help intensify the feeling of the poem.

Interestingly, some of the most profound and most often quoted sections of the Bible are boundaries. Eight of the Ten Commandments are boundaries of where not to go. St. Paul, in his letter to the Corinthians, defines love at least partly in terms of boundaries: "Love is not boastful, love is not jealous...."

There are, necessarily, sacrifices involved with self-discipline. Much as you may love your desserts or rich foods, if you want to stay healthy you'll probably have to forgo that pleasure more often than not. In this way, setting boundaries for yourself can force you to confront your true desires: is the goal really worth the sacrifice to you? If you really want to get fit and stay in shape, you don't need to fall for the fads and run out and buy the latest book on dieting. No matter how many books you buy, how many "weight loss" programs you join, or how much you spend on fitness equipment, you'll still need to learn to weigh the short-term, instant gratification that comes from eating whatever (and whenever) you want with the long-term objective of your good health and well-being. It also isn't realistic to think of fitness as simple weight loss from dieting. A healthy, balanced diet and a consistent exercise routine are the cornerstones of healthy living and they both require boundaries of "where not to go" as personal sacrifices you're willing to make in order to reach your goals.

After a clinic I often go out to dinner with the people who have organized the workshop and I can't tell you how many times I get offered another beer, or glass of wine, or a big fat rich dessert, and when I say "no thanks" I am met with disbelief. "Come on" they say, "look at you, you're so skinny you can afford to have another." Actually, I'm not skinny, I'm lean, and at my age, with all my old injuries and considering just how physical my work is, I need to stay in good shape in order to be able to do my job. What these people don't seem to get is that it's not because I'm "skinny" that I have room to say yes to their offer of extra calories, it's precisely because I have learned the value of saying no to the excesses, and because I do not let myself go without regular exercise, that I am able to keep myself in good shape.

And nothing will teach you faster about the need for boundaries and self-discipline than going into business for yourself. You will quickly discover the paradox that being your own boss means you've still got one. Or in my case, two—for Kathryn is every bit as committed to this work as I am. She's become my best apprentice and takes an important role in every clinic I run these days. With two of us working in harmony, urging each other on and keeping each other on track, the result is much more than a simple doubling of our business's human resources. As we feed off each other's ideas and enthusiasm, it's as if we have four times the energy and enthusiasm we did before. Like a horse and rider slowly becoming collected, as we learn to identify and respect each other's boundaries we make each other healthier, happier, and more productive. Simply put, we work like a team to make each other better.

It may seem like a long stretch from applying more boundaries to our horses to applying self-restraint, but it's not. I believe the two are intertwined. We simply can't bring discipline and collection to our mounts if we're confused in our own minds about our motives, methods, and goals. We must understand all three with crystal clarity, and that understanding is achieved only through a disciplined self-awareness. And once we know where we're going and why we want to get there, only discipline—setting boundaries for ourselves for where not to go—can see us through to achieving it.

[10]

calm and collected

$\mathcal{S}$EVEN CHAPTERS AGO I described how I left the home that Anita and I had created together and set out on the road on my own. I talked about how constant travel and the breakup of our marriage isolated me from what used to be my home base. I was always alone, either in my motor home or flying to the next round pen and riding arena on my marathon travel schedule. Cut off from anyone or anything that might help me stay grounded, my life became as fluid as a river. At times, it was desperately sad and lonely, but I had been freed from the tedious daily details of living that distract most of us. I became immersed in the world of my students. With little else to do as I traveled from one clinic to the next, my experiences with hundreds, even thousands of students sifted through my mind and eventually began to resolve themselves in a series of patterns.

Those patterns are what I've spent the last seven chapters describing. As a kind of mental shorthand, I've reduced each of them to a single word or phrase. There's alignment, forward, contact, timing, level, bend, more boundaries, and, finally, collection. Each one of these concepts encompasses patterns on its own—patterns of horse/human interaction and a pattern of echoes that ring through into the rider's life beyond the arena. But as I've hinted a time or two throughout this journey we've taken together, these eight concepts also work together to form a grander pattern. It's time to consider what this larger design really is.

I first called it "the eightfold path," a term I borrowed from Buddhism. The image of a path is useful because it conveys the idea of a journey, of getting closer and closer to a goal through the sustained application of effort. That's certainly true here and we don't want to lose sight of the fact that we are working toward a goal, but path imagery has its shortcomings. For example, you can start on a path from anywhere you find yourself on it. That's not the case here. There's no quality forward until at least a basic understanding of alignment has been achieved. Each concept is built on the foundation of the previous one, so maybe these concepts are better visualized as a pyramid.

But the pyramid brings its own problems. Once you've built a layer of the pyramid, you're finished with it. You're working on the next level now and the previous one is just the ground beneath your feet. You just don't think about it anymore. Clearly, that's not the case here either. We're all going to be working on even the most basic horse concepts as long as we're still riding, always trying to refine our alignment, always trying to get our timing even more accurate. In addition, these concepts not only build step-by-step, they also feed back into each other. Things we learn when we're working on bend will deepen our understanding of level. Once you feel even a moment of a horse beginning to develop self-collection, the contact will become as light as a feather and "feel" will take on a whole new meaning. Knowledge flows in all directions among all these concepts, so maybe the best image is of a web—but the web removes that idea of forward progress.

Path, pyramid, web—each of these visualizations of the process we're engaged in has its strengths and weaknesses. But having three mutually contradictory descriptions of what we're doing here doesn't help us understand it. It's just confusing.

I spent a lot of time on the road puzzling over this one. It may seem like a fruitless angels-on-the-head-of-a-pin kind of debate, but it's not. When you're a teacher, you realize how powerful metaphors can be. The wrong one—or the insufficiently correct one—can screw up a student (or a horse) for years. The right image, however, is like turning on a light bulb in a darkened room. Eventually, I think that the light-bulb came on for me. I'll tell you where the switch is in a little while, but first I need to lay a little groundwork.

Let's return to our basic eight concepts, however we visualize them. Each can be understood narrowly, as precise technical descriptions of something taking place in a round pen, riding arena, or wherever else interaction is taking place between human and horse. Alignment deals with the relative strategic positions of horse and human. Forward describes the fundamental movement we want to create in the horse. Contact tells us how to introduce boundaries that begin to focus and control that movement. Timing lays out when it is most or least advantageous to communicate that control. Level is about the physiological signs that tell us how the horse is reacting to the control we're beginning to establish. Bend refines our control with improved balance so we work with and not against the horse. And finally, more complex boundaries created by dynamic transitions and changes of intent encourage our horses to "carry themselves" and that refined control will build into the final concept of collection, which is what we're ultimately aiming for.

Clear equestrian goals, all of them. And all of them, in some form or other, have been developed and discussed in riding manuals and coaching sessions since the day five thousand years ago when some nomad on the steppes of Central Asia thought it might be worth giving his son a few hints on how to deal with these useful new creatures that were becoming so popular around the camp. For the well-being of our horses, these concepts should be as grounded in the day-to-day reality of horsemanship as proper feed and veterinary care. But they're not.

But I believe there is much more going on between humans and horses than just the art and science of horsemanship. Throughout the book, I've suggested that applying these concepts to working with your horse sets up a resonance in your heart that can echo in your life far beyond the barn and arena. Its time I explained why I think this is so.

As I've said before, horses don't make any distinction between how they feel and how they act. Their psychology is mirrored in their physiology and vice versa, to the point where it almost doesn't make sense to speak separately about the two. To borrow a phrase from my previous book, horses don't lie. It just isn't in them. In fact, dishonesty is so far out of the range of their experience that they can't imagine anyone else lying either. That means you. They make the same assumptions about you that they would make about another horse. That is, they think what you're saying is what you really mean— always keeping in mind that when we say "saying," we mean "saying with body language," which is the only language horses speak.

So when we combine that down-to-the-core frankness with the hypersensitive awareness that comes with prey consciousness, what do we get? We get a being that can size us up with a single look, and with unnerving accuracy. They hear your verbal commands, but they're really not that interested in them. What they care about is how you stand, how you walk, how you sit on their backs, and how you shape yourself every moment you're around them. In other words, a horse does not care where you're from, what you do for a living, how much money you make, what is the color of your skin, your age, your gender, or your political or religious beliefs. A horse is only concerned about how you behave. With horses, *who* you are is *how* you are. As the old horse industry cliché has it: A horse knows what you know.

We, however, have learned to devalue those body language signals in favor of words—a powerful and useful medium, but one that makes it much easier to disguise our true feelings. Our body language is just as honest as that of the horse; we've simply learned to disregard it. That may be just as well. It's hard to imagine civilized life if we were absolutely honest with each other all the time, and the white lie perhaps has its place ("The meal you served was delicious; I'm just not hungry…"). And as our civilization grows larger, more complex, and more impersonal, it becomes easier and easier to disguise what we're really thinking. But our true feelings remain mirrored by our bodies. Ask any cop who questions suspects or any lawyer who cross-examines witnesses: body language is a powerful way to determine if someone is telling the truth.

Horses, therefore, can read the truth about us. And here's the crucial step: They react to what they see. They give us feedback on what our bodies are telling them. Not what our lying mouths are saying, but our truthful bodies. If we know how to hear what the horses are saying, they will tell us what we are truly like.

When I write that horses need us to be consistent, confident leaders they can count on every single time, it's not just a piece of strive-for-excellence rhetoric. Remember the distance we're trying to travel with our horses. We're taking what is essentially a prey animal, a frightened, angry, or sullen victim living a neurotic life filled with attention deficit disorder, and trying to transform her into a calm, confident, focused athlete. If you are to give your horse the mindset of a champion, you have to develop one for yourself first. Horses really do need you to be that person, in a very literal sense. If you're not, if you're just putting on a show, if you're lying (even if only to yourself), they'll find out. This may sound too lofty, too idealistic for some people, but horses live in a world of lead, follow, or get out of the way. The sooner we stop denying what they really need from us, the better our chances of evolving past merely riding our pets and developing a truly mutually advantageous relationship with them.

The good news is that horses are generous. They'll forgive mistakes. They'll help us learn. We can use the feedback they give us to become the kind of people they need us to be—calm, focused, aware, confident, compassionate, and assertive without being threatening. And if we let them, they will bring us to an awareness of what's holding us back. They can help us to move forward by isolating and confronting our dysfunctions and our past traumas. God knows, I've had plenty of both in my life long before my heartbreaking episode with Stella, and it's always been the horses that got me through them. If we bring this approach into the arena with us, the eight concepts I've outlined in this book will burrow themselves deep in your psyche like a computer program. And yes, your operating system will be changed.

I believe that our bodies, our minds, and our spirits are all connected and they all need to be developed for us to go forward as balanced and centered human beings. Horses, because they read the truth of our souls in the orchestration of our gestures, are the surest aides I've found to accomplish this. I've felt this profoundly in my own life. And I've seen it work in the lives of hundreds of others that I've worked with. These ideas, I believe, are more than wispy new age wish fulfillment. They work—sometimes almost despite the best efforts of the human part of the equation to resist them.

Now, let's return to where we began this chapter. We left off at collection, the last of the eight concepts I've introduced. Here, we've taken the horse past simply being calm and are starting to build up energy, power, and agility in her body. The horse is relaxed but alert and ready for anything. By now, it should go without saying that you are, too. But there's collection and there's COLLECTION. It's an open-ended state and we can take it as far as we are able to. It's like karate or judo. There are black belts and there are tenth-degree black belts.

I make the comparison advisedly, because at this level I believe there are many similarities between equitation and the martial arts. Both offer mental and spiritual discipline. Both offer a way to unite body and mind. And both offer a spiritual path as well. Eastern disciplines such as tai chi, which is distilled from martial arts practice, are often undertaken as much for their value as active meditation as for

their physical benefits. Unfortunately, we in the West have
believe the East is the only place where such unity can be found, and
this Eastern link between body, mind, and spirit is almost a cliché in
Western culture. Remember the movie *The Karate Kid* with Ralph
Macchio or the TV show "Kung Fu," with David Carradine, the wandering warrior-priest who started out as "Grasshopper" snatching the
pebble from his master's hand?

I believe that we don't necessarily need to look East, or anywhere
else. We have a wonderful path available to us that couldn't be more
firmly rooted in our own culture. Horse play and horse sense can be
for us what martial arts are for a Zen master. In fact, sometimes I use
the term Equi-Zen for what I'm trying to express, not because I'm trying to push any one type of religion, but because I'm trying to encourage that type of awareness and that type of integration of the different
parts of our psyches to work in alignment with our bodies.

This dream of reconnection, of integration between our different
selves and with the world, is a very old one. It goes back to the Garden
of Eden, where Adam and Eve lived in perfect harmony with nature.
Ever since we were cast out for taking advantage of free rein to break
a boundary of where not to go, we've been looking for a way back in.
And in a small way, I believe that working with horses shows us a
back gate. I believe horses give us a chance to reassemble some of the
things that just haven't been holding together too well since that first,
fateful bite of the apple. I know, the ability to reverse the Fall of Man
is a tall claim to make for our relationship with a domesticated animal. But when you've seen people grow and change for the better as
they work with horses, it doesn't seem like too much of a stretch.

After all, let's not forget that it has been our relationship with
horses, and horsepower, that enabled us to explore new lands, defend
our homes, and conquer enemies. It was horsepower that fueled both
the agricultural and industrial revolutions. No other species on the
planet has been aligned with us to help develop our progress the way
horses have. We owe them a far greater debt of thanks than any other

creature with which we coexist. Dogs and cats are nice and life wouldn't be the same without them, but we didn't climb on their backs and harness their power to crawl from the caves to the sky-scrapers either. I'll bet more horses, millions of them, have died in our historic battles than all the men from all the armies put together.

This, however, does not mean we are trying to return the horse to its "natural" state or seeking some sort of "state of nature" with it. When I first began teaching some of what I'd learned about horse sense, there weren't very many of us around. In fact, it was considered kind of freakish to talk this way. Now, of course, after numerous pop-ular books, one of them mine (thanks, readers) and a blockbuster movie (Robert Redford's disappointing and distorted *The Horse Whisperer*), it's rare to find a horse trainer or clinician who hasn't adopted at least some of this kind of thinking. I don't and never did have a monopoly on equine insights. And while we each have our own signature style, like I said in the opening of this book, some of us are sincere shamans and some are mere showmen. And with so many false-prophets emerging since the book and movie *The Horse Whisperer,* I do find some of what's happening in the industry to be incredibly misleading.

The phrase "natural horsemanship," for example, is a dangerous oxymoron. It suggests that horses are fine as they are, that humans screw them up, and the trainer's job is to return the animal to its orig-inal state of grace. The problem here is that there is nothing natural about what we are doing. We are not only trying to convince prey ani-mals to allow predators on their backs and control their every move-ment, we are trying to get them to like it. Trying to pass this off as "natural" causes confusion that results in real physical consequences for both horse and rider. The natural conformation of a horse's back is inverted, not rounded. Some breeds are more naturally rounded than others, and alpha stallions and mares in the wild achieve that state for brief moments, but you will never see a consistently round-ed and collected horse cantering around in the wild. It emphatically is not natural. While it is vital to understand a horse's natural behavior, too much emphasis on the "natural" results in riders sitting atop inverted horses. That's bad for a horse, because its back then has less strength to carry the rider and is drastically inhibited from achieving maximum forward impulsion from its hindquarters. And it's bad for the rider, too.

Let me reiterate: We are not trying to create something natural here, or allow our horses to behave as they do out in the pasture. I don't want a natural horse; I want a supernatural horse. Horses are "naturally" flight animals—prey victims waiting to happen who get stressed out at the slightest noise or change in their environment. What we can and should do is tap into the natural psychology and etiquette of the herd. That allows us to pursue our own ends while keeping the horse's best interests in the forefront. That's quite different. We're saying, "I know you don't normally stay in this shape of relaxed, supple, collected movement, but that's what I want you to do because if you try it you'll find out how much better you can move and feel, even with me up here on your back. It's the best use of your mental and physical potential and it'll allow you to carry me confidently." We're using natural means, but to artificial ends. And as long as we keep the horse's best interests in the forefront, I believe that's how it should be. As James Agee has Katharine Hepburn say to Humphrey Bogart in *The African Queen*, "Nature...is what we are put into this world to rise above."

What a collected horse and rider are aiming to do is create a unit in which the body, mind, and spirit of both creatures are balanced and working together toward achieving maximum potential. The rider becomes a sort of benevolent shepherd to the horse and has its complete trust, while the horse becomes an agile and powerful companion, willing to help out with what the rider can't do for himself. In an earlier chapter, I briefly mentioned Hegel's ideas about how opposing forces resolve themselves into a higher synthesis. That's what happening here. Our ultimate goal is to resolve the predator and ＜

JIM KNELSON

Chris is well on his way to training Bahama, a thoroughbred x shire mare, into a "super-natural" horse.

ANITA IRWIN

Bahama and Chris—bonded, calm, and confident partners.

prey polarity. We have to understand it, embrace it, and we have to use it, but eventually we want to evolve beyond it. We want to create a new thing—a two-headed entity that has balanced its predator drive and aggression with the awareness and group-oriented mindset of prey consciousness.

Of course, the point I'm really trying to make here is that if we hope to develop the kind of integrity that leads to meaningful and lasting results, then whatever we do to the horse we must first create within ourselves. If we're going to be in that kind of partnership within the riding arena, we need to carry that kind of mental balance around with us everywhere we go. It's not something you can turn on and off—although I can't see why you'd want to. I think the world is desperate for people who can compete with each other without victimizing the loser, for people who can see past their own immediate needs, who can lead with the best interests of the herd at heart. In fact, I think this is the next step in human evolution.

It was when I was thinking through these issues that I finally hit upon the best way to describe the process engendered by the eight concepts. It's not a path, a pyramid, or a web. It's a spiral.

When viewed from the top, a spiral just looks like a circle. And there will be times when you feel as if that's what you're going around in. "Ah jeez, I thought I had this alignment stuff sorted out months ago," you'll moan as you realize that it's time yet again to revisit some fundamentals. This will happen over and over, probably with all eight concepts. But looked at from the side, the spiral goes up and up and up, constantly resolving opposites into new realities on a higher plane. And that is progress, real progress.

As I thought about my own past in those weeks and months after Stella threw all my preconceptions into disarray, I recognized some of those patterns in my own life. Time and again—I'm on my fourth marriage, after all—I've been knocked off my path by alignment that has gone awry. Over and over again, alignment gone bad has driven me toward more destructive behavior and caused me more grief than almost anything I could name. Relationships that seemed to promise mutual reinforcement turned out quite differently, and each time I've paid the price in anger, depression, frustration, and disillusionment. And each time, that has caused a part of me to rear up that I'd just as soon had stayed low and out of sight. The rage I felt in the round pen with Stella was only the most public and spectacular example. With Kathryn, however, something's different. I feel I've finally got it right, and it was how she learned to react with "horse sense" to the many difficult challenges of being my mate (what an understatement) that allowed me to discover the freedom to become proactive with my healing instead of reactive. As our work with our horses and students carried over into our relationship, Kathryn and I found ourselves "round-penning" each other through our issues instead of reacting to each other as predators that "go for the throat." It was this paradigm shift from "cat and mouse" behavior to "being the best horses that we could be" in my closest relationship that allowed room for me to feel vulnerable and still move forward. That, I believe, is what finally allowed me to make the breakthrough I did that will allow me to stay level-headed and compassionate as I find myself dealing with the Stellas of the world.

You may find yourself stuck in a similar cycle, dealing yet again with an issue related to contact or timing or bend. But every time you return to your old nemesis, you'll do so a bit smarter, with a higher awareness. You'll be able to look back at where you were, like a hiker climbing mountain switchbacks can look down on where he's come from.

Or if you prefer more down-to-earth language, maybe the whole process is like a wagon wheel rolling down the trail. The wheel has eight spokes, the eight paths we've been going over, and each of these spokes is connected to the hub of the wheel. The hub of the wheel is Awareness, where every spoke has its source and comes together with the other spokes for balance and support. The rim of the wheel also holds the spokes together but is not the source of the spokes. Rather, it is the direction in which the eight spokes are reaching out. The rim can be seen as such necessary life skills as consistency, patience, proactivity, decisiveness, composure, and the ability to multitask. This wheel of life, with its hub of self-awareness, branches out into the eight spokes of alignment, forward, contact, timing, level, more boundaries, and then collection. It is all held together with a rim made up of a myriad of life skills. As the wheel rolls forward, each one of these concepts bears the weight of that progress at different times. But each time the wheel revolves it carries us a little farther down the road.

The human-horse partnership, however, is not an equal one. Make no mistake about it, our horses need far more from us than do our dogs and cats. You can be a big softy and be pals with your dog or cat and let them run up and jump on you, bump into you, or ignore your commands and basically do whatever they want. You can even do this with your kids if you want. But keep in mind that first of all dogs and cats are predators and are much more naturally aligned with our innate behavior and body language. Second, our dogs and cats are a fraction of the size of our horses and we don't risk our lives by climbing on their backs and expecting them to let us control their direction. In short, the realities between horses and humans are worlds apart, but we ask far more of them than any other animal because we like to ride them. We assume more risks with horses than with any other animal on the planet. Just look at what happened to Christopher Reeve. Horses are magnificent creatures that offer us a unique window into our souls and an opportunity to develop them, but we can't ever lose sight of the fact that, ultimately, they are potentially very volatile and dangerous and they look to us for leadership. That means that while we may ride them into collection and travel a long way with them on the journey, there's one more step the human has to take. If we want the type of leadership I've been talking about, there's only one way to convince the horse to give it to us. Restraints won't do it, spurs and big, punishing bits won't do it, bribing them with carrots won't do it, and trying to communicate with them from

the heart on some sort of psychic level won't do it. There's only one
pillar this kind of leadership can rest on: the rider's own integrity.   <

Think about the integrity of a wheel. If the hub of the wheel,
awareness, isn't solid and substantial, it can't support the spokes and
soon the wheel falls apart. True, if any of the spokes are not balanced,
the wheel wobbles and it wanders off track. And if the rim is com-
promised—if we lose our patience or become reactive—then again,
the wheel veers off course and we hit the ditch. Who knows, maybe
this is where people struggling to recover from alcoholism or substance addiction came up with the term "falling off the wagon." My
point here is that no one spoke is more important than the others, and
the spokes go nowhere without the support of the rim. But everything
in the wheel revolves around and depends upon the hub of awareness.
Awareness is at the very center of our wheel of life, so how much
progress we make is directly related to the strength and size of that
hub. Leaders are big wheels and big wheels keep on turning.

Becoming a well-balanced wheel in order to develop the kind of
integrity a horse will respond to will eventually require us to come to
grips with our own deepest contradictions. There's no other way. It's
like the old joke about what you have to know to teach school: one
thing more than the students. This final step is the one thing that
Stella was determined to teach me. Just as we've balanced out predator and prey, we now have to look within and discover how to find
balance between our outward selves and personalities and our inner
selves, our Shadow sides.

[11]

the shadow rears
its ugly head

$\mathcal{E}$VERY NOW AND then, the world of pop culture trips over the
equine world and people who normally couldn't tell a Morgan
from a mustang start taking an interest in things horsey. Feature stories start popping up in newspapers and magazines and "color pieces"
air on the TV news. It happened during the whole horse whisperer
craze in the late 1990s, it happened with the book and movie
Seabiscuit, and it happened again in the spring of 2004 with a horse
by the pleasantly cheeky name of Smarty Jones.

Smarty Jones was a three-year-old thoroughbred when he came
into his fifteen minutes of fame, and a great fifteen minutes it was.
Nobody could resist his story.

That story began in 2001 when Smarty's owners, Roy and Pat
Chapman, followed the advice of their trainer and bred a recently
acquired mare to a stallion he had picked out. Smarty was the foal.
But nine months after Smarty's birth, the trainer and his wife were
found shot to death; their son was eventually sentenced to twenty-
eight years in prison for the crime. Emotionally devastated and concerned about Roy's health, the Chapmans sold off nearly all of their
horses. Smarty was one of only four they held on to.

That is surely enough tragedy to cling to any horse, but fate wasn't finished with Smarty Jones yet. During training, while his handlers were working with him on learning to enter the starting gate, Smarty reared up and smashed his head on an iron bar on the way down. Those who saw the accident said the then-two-year-old was unconscious for thirty seconds and was so badly hurt internally that he was bleeding from the nostrils. One trainer thought he was dead. Smarty fractured his skull and nearly lost his left eye.

Nevertheless, neither Smarty nor the Chapmans gave up. Smarty spent months in rehab and healed well. So well, in fact, that in his track debut on November 9, 2003, he won his race by nearly eight lengths. Two weeks later, he won his sophomore effort by an incredible fifteen lengths. Track insiders starting talking, and the buzz only got louder on May 1, 2004, when Smarty won the 130th running of the Kentucky Derby. So far, it was only a story in the horse world. But two weeks later, Smarty Jones became a household name when the Preakness Stakes became his sixth straight victory, giving him the first two jewels of the Triple Crown. No horse had claimed that prize in twenty-five years. Winning it would earn the Chapmans, who had refused all offers for the horse that was one of their last links to their murdered trainer and friend, a record six million in purses and bonuses.

All the elements were in place: an underdog horse from a loyal mom-and-pop stable, a tragedy, a gutsy recovery, and the biggest, fattest, juiciest pot of gold ever at the end of the thoroughbred racing rainbow. If you made up a story like that, people would roll their eyes in disbelief. But for Smarty, it was all true, and sports reporters more accustomed to transcribing quotes from basketball players brushed up their Racing Form lingo to put Smarty all over North America's front pages.

It was a great story. And it was great timing, too. The United States was just beginning to realize that the invasion of Iraq wasn't going to be quite the cakewalk it had been sold as. Doubts were creeping in as body bags filtered home. America's economy was looking shaky, too, as jobs increasingly fled overseas. The news was bad, and when the news is bad, editors go looking for a pleasant distraction to cheer their readers up. Smarty Jones was it. He was everywhere.

During that spring of horse racing fever, I picked up one of those front pages. It was ESPN sports magazine, one of the most widely circulated on the continent. And there was Smarty on the cover. At a casual glance, he looked as if he was living up to his name—all big teeth and goofy, horsey grin. The caption was suitably witty: "Will Smarty get the last laugh?" But something in the picture didn't seem right. I took a closer look.

That big smile, so jaunty and apparently heart-warming, was produced by a lip chain. Lip chains are good-sized steel links that go under the horse's top lip and yank it back to expose its teeth and put direct pressure against the gums. It's an incredibly severe tool that, sadly, is used as a form of restraint too often with horses by far too many people. From amateurs to pros, veterinarians to farriers, wrapping a chain around a horse's nose and, even worse, through his or her mouth, is a cruel but too-common practice found not just at the track but in every segment of the horse industry. Smarty's eyes were bugged out and glazed with indignance and his ears were pinned almost flat back in anger. This was America's hero. This was the story that was supposed to make us feel good. This was supposed to be an equine version of the old ya-gotta-believe-in-miracles, underdog-makes-good American myth. I looked at the picture, and I saw a slave in chains.

Why bring up Smarty Jones? Not, certainly, to criticize the Chapmans. They stuck with that horse and I was as sorry for them as anyone when their spunky little horse got beat in the Belmont later that season. Nor am I trying to suggest that Smarty was being abused. I'm sure that a six-million-dollar horse gets treated very well, although I wonder about the ethics of putting him in distress just to get a snappy magazine shot. This isn't about horse owners or horse races or even about the media. This is about us, and our ability to live in denial. I showed that picture to lots of my friends and they all laughed and smiled with variations on, "How 'bout that Smarty Jones? And that's a great picture. It really sums up the whole classic story." It's like when people applaud a so-called natural horseman riding around bareback and bridleless on a horse whose body language is screaming unhappiness. We see what we want to see and believe what we want to believe, even when the truth is staring us in the face.

When this race horse, a thoroughbred chesnut mare, was handed to Chris by her trainer during a demonstration at Keeneland race track in Lexington, Kentucky, she already had a chain over her nose because she was dangerously aggressive and "out of hand." As Chris first begins to work with the mare she is indeed a handful, throwing her head violently into the air and often shouldering into Chris to push him around.

KATHRYN KINCANNON-IRWIN

The mare quickly responds and becomes level-headed and "in hand" as she sees and feels how Chris uses assertive but non threatening prey body language to channel her movement instead of passive-aggressive predator body language to lead her around by her nose.

KATHRYN KINCANNON-IRWIN

Within minutes of being handled by Chris, the mare has gone from difficult to dreamy and Chris has taken the chain off of her nose, hopefully once and for all.

It should be clear by this point in the book that "training" horses
is a long process of clarification: making sure our horses know who is
in charge, relaying unambiguous messages in an assertive but nonthreatening manner, and being consistent with them. We need our
horses to gradually let go of lingering fears, angers, and suspicions
that cloud their ability to respond to our intent without restraint. It
should also be clear by this point that if we want to create that state
in the horse, we need to create it in ourselves. We need to see clearly,
understand accurately, and respond appropriately. That picture of
Smarty Jones is an example of how often we choose to do just the
opposite. It was intended to sell us on the storyline. It had nothing to
do with what the horse was actually feeling. Smarty Jones is an example of how we paper over dysfunction with "The Big Lie."

Let me give you another example. In the fast-growing field of
equine-assisted psychotherapy, or EAP, there are more and more mental health therapists and counselors now working with horses as an
"alternative experience" to try to make headway with people who are
stuck and not making much progress with conventional modes of
therapy. In my last book I talked a bit about my role within this
movement. I've been working with therapists practicing EAP in
developing a basic competency in horse-handling skills that guarantee the best interests and nature of the horses. After all, how shallow
and sadly ironic it would be if when we offer a feel-good experience
for people, no matter how badly they need it, the bedside manner of
the therapist or the client/patient inadvertently leaves the horses
experiencing confusion, fear, anger, or sullenness? Anyway, I seemed
to have struck a chord with *Horses Don't Lie,* and I started getting
more and more requests to work as a consultant with the healers
attempting to work together with horses and people in therapy. One
of the calls I received was from a "boys' ranch" in the American
MidWest where approximately seventy young male "offenders"
between the ages of thirteen and seventeen live together in group
homes.

At first glance the ranch was a paradise. The grounds were green and immaculately landscaped, looking far more like a country club than a facility that housed some of the toughest young men from the turbulent streets of the inner city. These boys had all been too young for jail, but they had also proven to be too violent for juvenile hall, so the court had ordered them to do their time at the ranch. The place was first class, with beautiful big ranch-style homes that would be the envy of any executive. There were eight to ten boys to a home and each house had a live-in husband and wife team of counselors that played the roles of Mom and Dad. The ranch was out in the woods, in the middle of nowhere, with everything a young man could ask for. Everything, that is, except girls, booze, and drugs. The facility had a high school as well as a woodworking shop, automotive shop, and commercial kitchen where the boys could not only finish their education but also receive vocational training that would hopefully help them find a job once they were released back into the real world. There was a great gymnasium, volleyball and basketball courts, and—you guessed it—a barn full of horses and an outdoor and indoor riding arena. The philosophy was to show the boys that if they worked hard and played by the rules, there was an alternative to the mean streets and that their lives could indeed become much more rewarding if they toed the line. One more thing—the ranch is run by Christians and prayer and church attendance is mandatory.

On my first day at the ranch, I was taken on a tour and given the standard orientation. The first thing that struck me was that I saw a framed print of the same painting in each of the boys' homes and in each and every building on the property. These were all copies of a huge mural that had been painted in the dining hall, dominating the entire room for all to see. The image was of four horses, all different colors, running wild and free, full of spirit, in a high meadow full of wildflowers. The herd was surrounded by snow-capped mountains as they galloped below thunderclouds with an enormous rainbow arching across the sky. The title of the painting was "Memories of

Freedom." So what's my point? Well, during orientation the boys find out, as I did, that the painting is actually a memorial and that the horses had lived there at the ranch and had died a horrible death just a few years earlier in a barn fire. Now just hold that thought for a few minutes.

After I've finished the tour I'm asked how I'd like to begin my work with the counselors and the horses and I say that I'd like to observe a session where a therapist would be working with one of the boys and a horse. They agreed and set up the session. The therapist brought a young man into the arena where a lone horse was standing off in the far corner looking sullen and disinterested. The boy looked bewildered and somewhat nervous but he was still trying to act cool. The therapist then told the boy that today, instead of their regular chat in his office, they were going to work with the horse and he asked the kid if this was okay. The boy just shrugged his shoulders and said, "Whatever." What I saw next shocked and angered me. The therapist handed this city kid, who had no experience with horses, a halter and told him to go catch the horse and lead him back to the gate where the three of us were standing. The boy looked puzzled but he did as he was told and sauntered across the arena toward the horse. The horse, being savvy about halters, of course saw a predator coming straight at his head to capture him and he trotted off, avoiding being caught while tossing his head at the boy, basically telling the boy to "get lost." The boy slumped his shoulders and sulked back to us, dejected, dropped the halter on the ground, and said, "The stupid horse didn't wanna be caught." The counselor was actually grinning about this and said to him, "And how does it make you feel that the horse didn't want to be with you?" Again, the boy just shrugged and said, "Whatever. I don't care."

At this point the counselor looked at me and told me that this is when the therapy would usually begin and they would "process" the feelings of anger, blame, denial, sadness, or whatever reactions were triggered within the boys if and when the horses rejected them like this.

This, as far as they were concerned, was the first lesson. I said I'd seen enough, and I thanked the young man for allowing me to observe.

Then I called all the counselors together for a meeting. When I had the group of would-be healers together I asked them if any of the boys at the ranch had ever commented that the horse stalls in their new barn (recently built to replace the one destroyed in the fire) reminded them of jail cells? They all looked at me with mild surprise and said that yes, as a matter of fact, that's usually exactly what the boys said when they came into the barn for the first time. "Okay," I said, "so you can appreciate that these boys, after seeing how the horses live 'in jail' would easily relate to them." They nodded their heads. "Now you're probably not going to like what I have to say next, but here it is. I can relate to these boys because I come from a background similar to theirs and as far as I'm concerned, and I'd be willing to bet that as far as they're concerned, your program has no credibility whatsoever. I bet they think it's a joke. You're kidding yourself if you think you'll really get anywhere with these kids because they see your entire approach to them as one big lie after another." Their leader asked me what I meant by this. I said, "You're obviously very proud of that painting called 'Memories of Freedom,' but the boys have put two and two together and they know it's a lie. They know those horses never once lived free, they know those poor animals died a horrible death, trapped in 'prison,' unable to escape to save themselves while the barn burned down around them. But the phony story you tell won't even allow them to feel the truth. Then you add insult to injury by telling them that the work they do with the horses is for their own good, but the first thing you do is set them up for failure. When you send a boy out to 'catch' a horse he has no history with, without any knowledge as to how best to approach a horse, you're basically telling him that its okay to victimize another being. Isn't that just perpetuating the same vicious cycle that brought them here?"

The group was stunned and not one of them said a word. They just sat there staring at me in disbelief, their denial written all over their faces. After all, they were the good guys, Christians out to save the world, and these were the bad boys from the mean streets. Why was I pointing a finger at them? I asked them to consider another approach. "What if you were straight up and honest with these guys? Why not tell them that yes, these box stalls are indeed jail cells for horses and no, the horses in the painting never did enjoy their freedom. Don't you realize that these boys, even if it's at a level that they're not conscious of, most likely feel that they have more in common with the horses at the ranch than they do with you counselors, their teachers, or the house parents? The adults working at this facility are all free to come and go but the horses and the boys are stuck here together, in jail, albeit a very cozy place to be penned up. Why not tell the boys that instead of therapy you'd like to know if they are open to making life a little easier and hopefully more enjoyable for their fellow inmates, the horses? Instead of setting them up for failure and then processing how they feel about being a loser, why not ask them if they'd like to learn how to handle, train, and perhaps ride the horses? My guess is that most of them would rather be in the arena playing with horses than in the kitchen washing dishes or in the garage changing the oil in a car. And if the boys do indeed willingly sign on to learn about the horses, you've got them right where you should really want them. You've got them voluntarily asking to learn something new and this is exactly what these kids need, because learning how to train horses first and foremost involves self-awareness and this becomes a process for learning how to learn. Just think of all the life skills these kids could discover within themselves and develop if you were open and honest with them and gave them the chance to learn how to play horse games by horse rules instead of setting them up for failure!"

When I was done, one therapist broke down in tears, one stormed out of the room in a huge huff, two of them stared at me like I was from Mars, and one said, "I hear you Chris, so show us where to go from here." I spent the next three days teaching these people, these would-be mentors to disadvantaged youth, how to rise to the occasion of being the best horses that they could be. As it turns out, the one who stormed out of the meeting was the so-called "horse expert" of the bunch, and he threatened to resign if they intended to follow my foolishness. He no longer works there. And the one who broke down in tears came up to me after my final day of work at the ranch and told me she had a confession to make. It turned out that she had read *Horses Don't Lie* before I got there. When she learned that I had turned my back on Christianity because of all the hypocrisy I had found in organized religion, she decided that it was her divine mission to bring me back to the flock. In her mind, the horses at their barn had problems that needed to be fixed and I needed to find my way back to Christ and she was going to see to both. She then told me that after our three days of working together, she saw what healing was possible and what progress could be made if only she opened her mind to the possibilities of a new way to work with horses. She realized she was the one with problems and needed training, not the horses. But what really surprised me was when she told me that even though I had walked away from the church, I had in fact been far more of a Christian in my actions, while she had been judgmental, intolerant, and hypocritical. Wow, all that from delving into prey consciousness!

Learning to recognize and expose our lies is the final step we must take before we truly earn the right to tell our horses that we are their leaders. It's also, I believe, the final and essential step we must take before we can take any kind of reins of leadership with confidence and integrity. If we need to see clearly, understand accurately, and respond appropriately with our horses (or our children, our students, our staff), we have to first do so with ourselves.

All of us have characteristics that we don't like to own up to. If they're stubborn enough and stick around long enough, we try to finesse them away and pretend that they're not really us, just something we picked up along the way like a burr on a saddle blanket. That extra weight we can't seem to drop, even though we know it's damaging our health? We'll get rid of it someday. That cigarette habit that keeps coming back? We can quit any time. After all, we're not really overweight or tobacco addicts. It's just a phase. It's not the real us.

It's easy to pick on smokers and couch potatoes, but this insight cuts a little deeper than that. Recognize any of these? "I don't have a temper. That waitress deserved to get yelled at." "I know my credit is a little tight right now, but that blouse was a great deal and I can afford it." "I'm not afraid of commitment. I just don't think two years of dating is enough time to know if I'm ready to get serious." Try to come up with some yourself. It's easy and fun to play—and the examples you come up with might tell you some interesting things about yourself.

The point is that we have to stop living with self-delusions, putting on a lip chain and pretending it's a smile. Real problems have real causes and if we want to stop making excuses and telling lies we have to acknowledge them, just as we've learned to look for the real cause when our horses refuse to get into a trailer. I'm no psychologist, but I've learned from my own experience that we don't behave badly just for the hell of it. There's almost always something unresolved at the core of such problems, and we can't solve them just by stuffing our anger, pain, hurt, and frustration away in some dark mental corner. If we want our horses to stop running away from us or running over us and calmly face and focus on us, we have to face those parts of ourselves that we're not so proud of and that we'd prefer others didn't see. We already know that horses can see them. News flash: everyone else can see them, too. It's only ourselves that we're fooling.

This, I believe, is a serious problem in the world we've created for ourselves. This self-delusion is at the heart of the inconsistent, hypocritical behavior we see all around us, including in our leaders. Everywhere we look there is a crisis in leadership. None but the naïve look for heroes in the sports world anymore. The days of Muhammad Ali and Jackie Robinson are long gone and today a pro athlete is considered a role model if he wins games and stays out of court. Religious leaders? A seemingly unending series of child abuse revelations, in communities as remote as Inuvik in Canada's Northwest Territories and as central as Boston, have forever shaken our trust in men wearing robes.

Back in the '90s, entrepreneurship was considered next to godliness. But by the time the decade was over, businesspeople at the top of the so-called New Economy had revealed they had the business ethics of a small-time drug dealer. Nobody even expects political speeches to be meaningful, or inspirational, or challenging. Reassuring and bland is good enough. When politicians do turn to action, we've long ago grown suspicious of whether things really are done of the people, by the people, and for the people. And the media, those whom we trust to ferret out the truth, have badly damaged themselves with case after case of getting things wrong or simply making things up. That's when they're not busy being hired messengers regurgitating the latest press releases from the corporate and political powers that be or simply trying to shout each other down on TV.

Integrity is in short supply and few leaders seem able to walk the talk. It's as if these people, these leaders in positions of power and authority, are at war with themselves. They wind up doing the opposite of what they say they're going to do. They exploit those they claim to protect, lie when they promise truth, and pocket the resources they claim to have created for others. From somewhere deep inside themselves, they constantly sabotage their own best motives.

I believe that for many of us, sabotage is what is happening. We've denied so many parts of ourselves. We push all that "bad" stuff down, lock it in a stall and hobble it. We don't even try to understand it. And because we don't know it very well, it can take us by surprise, rearing its ugly head and screwing us up when we least expect it. I call those parts of us our Shadow selves. I've got one, too. Let me tell you a bit it about it.

Me and my Shadow actually have a long history together, dating back to my youth in a very rough working class neighborhood in

St. Catharines, Ontario, and later in the more sedate Swift Current, Saskatchewan. I won't talk too much about my youth here (I wrote about it in my first book), but I will say that I did not have a model childhood. By the ripe old age of seven, I'd realized that my parents resented each other, they resented the burden of children, and they resented their jobs. Wrapped up in their own pain and substance abuse, they weren't really aware of me. Aside from the beatings he used to inflict upon me on a regular basis, my stepdad constantly belittled and ridiculed me when I couldn't do simple things like catch a ball, but it never occurred to either him or my mom to have my eyes checked. I was nine years old before a teacher at school noticed me squinting to see the blackboard and finally realized that I probably needed glasses. My vision was so bad I was legally blind. For the first nine years of my life, I was like a blind rabbit in a house full of wolves.

I think now that it may have been those vision problems that caused me to withdraw into myself from a world that I couldn't quite bring into focus. This outsider stance gave me a perspective from which to look at other people's lives, and even as a boy it seemed to me that most people were just going through their daily routines, like petting zoo ponies that walk around the same circle day after day. And the more I looked at people, the more I realized how different their actions were from their words, and how ready they were to deny their contradictions and betrayals.

When I was in early grade school, I used to go after school to the home of a teenage boy who lived around the corner until my parents got home from the bar they frequented after their days at work. The young man was a child molester—although I was too young to really understand what he was doing. One afternoon, we were up in his bedroom and he was up to his tricks. Then, without warning, his father walked in on us. He looked at us and what his son was doing, then walked out without saying a word. The look on his face is what I remember: anger, fear, and guilt. He knew that his son was only practicing on me what had been done to him. I couldn't have expressed it at the time, but that afternoon planted the seed for everything I needed to know about how dysfunction gets handed down from one generation to the next.

Virtually every authority figure I looked to for guidance let me down. My teachers were either apathetic, control freaks, or well-meaning but simply clueless about how to reach me. In the search for some kind of authenticity, I joined the Boy Scouts, and for a while I loved the organization's values of integrity and honor. I made it to the top, the Canadian equivalent of an Eagle Scout, called a Senior Sixer. But even the Boy Scouts turned out to be simply a cover for more lies when a local official was revealed to be a pedophile.

So I grew into an introspective, brooding kid. In athletics, I shied away from games like hockey or football that demanded aggressive conflict; I got more than enough of that at home. I found I was best at what I now refer to as "prey consciousness" sports, and found a kind of deliverance in transcending boundaries of physical pain and endurance. In St. Catharines, for a few years I won gold medals for rowing, winning both the Canadian high school nationals and the prestigious Royal Canadian Henley. In Ontario, I won award after award from the provincial government for my "outstanding athletic achievements" and when my family moved west to Swift Current, Saskatchewan, I went out for track and won ribbons and smashed regional records in middle- and long-distance running. I was very, very good at enduring the burn, learning how to control my breath and emotions while embracing the pain of driving my body further and harder, always onward to victory. I was obsessed with winning and thereby proving to my parents that despite what they told me I was indeed good for something. When at home, I would hide in my room and pour my heart into my guitar. I consistently won music and talent contests and I sang in the school choir. And I asked my lonely questions in search of answers that offered some sense and meaning to my desperate life. I didn't ask, however, what all that deception around me and disillusion inside me was doing to me. I didn't know that they would nurture anything bad.

Then I met a girl. Sandy had many of the same questions I did, and she had found some answers in Christianity. As our relationship grew, I came to accept some of those same answers. I became a Christian.

Then one day, for no reason that I could understand, Sandy stopped returning my phone calls. I couldn't reach her for several days, and then I had a dream. After that dream, I knew where she was. I called the hospital and sure enough, there she was. She had had an abortion. I was furious with her and demanded to know how she could have destroyed our child until she silenced me with the revelation that the baby hadn't been mine. To this day, I can't really describe the hurt. I

Chris with his crew from West Park High School in St. Catharines, Ontario, winners of the 1975 Canadian National High School Rowing Championship. Chris, age 15, is fourth from left, holding the trophy.

was humiliated. I felt like a fool, and as I wandered around in a daze, my wounded pride festered in me like an unattended welt. I'd suffered plenty of deception in my life, but this felt like everything else all rolled into one, leaving me with a tightly coiled ball of ugliness in the pit of my stomach. Then I ran into Sandy's mother in a local mall, and that black ball slowly unraveled. Sandy's mom was a loving and caring woman, a true and fine example of a Christian who did indeed walk her talk, and I had always enjoyed my conversations with her. I told her the whole story: what our relationship had been like, what her daughter was going through, and what she had revealed to me. If I'd been shocked, Sandy's mother felt the earth open under her feet and swallow everything she thought she knew.

I walked away trying to convince myself what I'd just said and done had been in Sandy's best interest. But the more I thought about it, the more I realized I'd done it simply to be cruel, to make Sandy and those close to her suffer the way I had. I'd never sought to deliberately hurt someone before, and for a kid who maybe thought too much and lived too much inside his own head the realization that I had deviously wrapped up my need for revenge in what I pretended to be sincere concern was crushing. I'd sworn to myself never to pass on the victimization I had experienced so much of. Yet here I'd gone and done just that, deliberately. I was ashamed. I desperately wanted to root this ugliness out of my personality forever. Following up my newfound Christian beliefs, I decided the way to purify myself was to study for the ministry. To prepare myself, I visited a monastery near Saskatoon, Saskatchewan. Those kind, wise monks recognized my intent and took me in.

As you may have concluded by now, I'm a bit of an extremist. It wasn't enough for me to simply meditate and pray. I had to fast. And the regular type of fast the monks recommended, in which you drink juice but eat no food, wasn't good enough. I felt that I was so bad I had to deny myself everything but water. By the fifth or sixth day of my fast, I was in a totally altered state. It was, I thought, wonderful. I'd never been so sure of anything as I was of Jesus's love and my closeness to him. To say I felt washed clean doesn't come close to describing it. I felt so pure that even the thought of succumbing to that dark side of myself ever again seemed impossible. I would never go there again.

The last morning of my fast I was praying in the chapel, bathing in God's glory and my newfound goodness. I was staring up at the crucifix, intent on the face of the meek and suffering Jesus. I felt I had his strength within me now and it made me, in a strange sort of way, cocky. I was practically challenging Satan, imagining I was now far beyond both his power and my own darkness.

Suddenly, the crucifix began to change and distort. I knelt, unable to move, as the sculptor's image of Christ gradually changed into a hideous, grinning demon. What had been the body of Christ got down off the cross and walked toward me, growing more grotesque with every step. He stuck his face right up to mine. "Do not mock me," he hissed. I had come face to face with my Shadow.

If extreme hunger can produce hallucinations, that was a particularly powerful one. Scared and shaken to the core, I ended my fast that day and I left the monastery soon after. I thought I had banished my Shadow, but it had been waiting for me all along. I didn't know what to do. In confusion, I quit school, ran away from my family once and for all, left everything behind me, took my aching heart and hit the road.

I did my best to forget those weeks. I buried the humiliation Sandy had made me feel. I never thought about the Shadow's terrifying response to my prideful challenge that morning in the chapel. And the intoxicating life I soon found, bouncing back and forth between riding stables and ski resorts, certainly made it easy to forget everything in the past and focus on the enjoyment of the moment. I thought I could just stay on the surface of life and never have to go back to that dark place within myself. Most of the time I did pretty well. But while you can run, you can't hide. Eventually, I got myself into a spot that convinced me that I had something seriously out of balance within me.

Meanwhile, although I passed a few pleasant years this way and eventually went to Nevada, where I kept on training horses and skiing. It was a free-and-easy life, full of free-and-easy people. It seemed as if everyone I met was either on holiday or had so much money that work was optional, and it was party, party, party. There were a lot of cocaine cowboys around in those days and "blow" was everywhere. The manager of the ranch were I worked did a lot of it, and whenever he came around he'd bring a nice big bag of white powder. It didn't take me long to acquire the taste. I lived like that for months, then I had the severe riding accident I mentioned earlier that laid me out. I spent that winter recuperating at the ranch owner's house, which was very kind of him. But between the heavy-duty prescription painkillers I was on and the constant cocaine-powered social scene I frequented, I soon became hooked on the cocaine.

Some of you might wonder how an eagle scout/award-winning athlete could have ever been open to even trying cocaine in the first place. It's a tough question. Suffice it to say that when you grew up the way I did and almost all of the adults around you appeared to be liars and hypocrites, then everything that they tell you becomes suspect. When you're that young and wounded, if the people you don't respect or trust say, "Just say no," while all the cool and hip people you admire are having a blast saying "Yes, let's do another line," well, you throw caution to the wind and you experiment. I was veering from extreme to extreme, from trying to be a good Christian to getting my girlfriend pregnant, from fasting in a monastery to snorting coke. I thought authenticity and truth could only be found on the edge of things. I've always taken big risks, and cocaine, I guess, was just another of them.

I went back to work that spring, but now I was high all the time. I worked with the horses, I kept pushing myself with what was becoming known as extreme skiing, (jumping off cliffs and cornices, spending as much time up in the air on my skis as I did on the snow), and I partied and partied. Three years passed in a blur of horses and

RICK DEVIN

Chris, on the left, age 24, revealing his dark side during his cocaine cowboy days in the early 1980s.

snow—both kinds. I was having lots of fun and thrills and that's about all that mattered. In those three years, I doubt if Sandy or the demon from the chapel crossed my mind a half-dozen times. I thought I had successfully run away from the whole issue. Then, unsurprisingly, business at the riding stable where I worked at Lake Tahoe started to go bad. The stables closed due to soaring insurance premiums and I lost my job. I found another as a nightclub bouncer and wound up even more heavily into cocaine. I started dealing it in a small way to friends, and inevitably went into debt to another dealer with gang affiliations. I had to sell my saddle and my horse to save my skin. The horse I sold was T.C., the horse who started it all for me. In my humiliation and heartbreak, I realized I had to do something, but what I did was to go on one last binge. I woke up the next morning on a golf course, covered with mud and blood. I had no idea where my truck was or how I got there. It was my twenty-fifth birthday and on a day that should've been a happy one, the loss of T.C. due to my own pathetic behavior was just too much too ignore. I hated myself for having to sell him to pay off a drug debt. I quit cocaine that day and I've been clean of it ever since.

Shortly after that, my then-wife Robin came into a small inheritance and we decided to open a guest ranch together. Up until this point, horses had been my living, but I'd been too busy partying and running away from things to truly do them justice. Now, horses became my life. I became more and more interested in what they were doing, why they were doing it, and what it meant. This was almost twenty years ago, and it is when I laid the groundwork for everything I've done since.

But in a way, the horses became just another religious pilgrimage, just another drug I was addicted to. Sure, as an avoidance strategy it was a lot healthier than the previous ones I'd chosen. At least I was losing myself in something positive for both myself and other people. Nevertheless, for all my success with horses and even with my students, it took me a long time to understand that there was still a Shadow inside me. I could feel it prancing sometimes, when a horse or a client tried my patience or pushed my authority too hard. I felt it resurface years later with my kids, especially with my boy, Adler, when he pushed all my buttons about what it means to truly be a good father to a son. I'd get short, throttling down my anger. I swore to myself that no matter how challenging it got to raise our kids, they would never suffer from their father the way I did from mine. Although the cycle of family abuse stopped with me, I was still emotionally stuck in the mud. I was still hobbling that Shadow instead of listening to it, still restraining my demons instead of working with them out in the open. I guess I'd forgotten the lesson I should have learned years ago in that Saskatchewan chapel. I thought I could nurture my good self and suppress my bad. I thought I'd crush it as if it didn't exist. I thought if I just kept a lip chain on my own dark side, it would be enough.

And it was, I suppose. Until Stella roared into the round pen in front of me.

[12]

the buck stops here

$\mathcal{J}$T'S BEEN A long, complicated path, full of detours and (I hope) insights, but we have at last returned to the dilemma that spurred the writing of this book: my battle with Stella.

That battle left me bruised in body, mind, and spirit. My body wasn't really much of a problem. Although I walked around pretty gingerly for a few days after those hours in the round pen with Stella, like a horse, I have adapted to my physical reality and learned how to heal on the run. I do owe a debt of thanks, however, to that big, bold, black Friesian stallion in Toronto who was the first horse I worked with after my war with Stella. His name is Jay and he was my saving grace. I couldn't have found myself working with a more perfect horse to start me off on my road to recovery after Stella. Although he was very macho and full of himself, and he played the horse games with fire and intensity, he was proud and athletic but he was not a bully. He was a "maybe" horse who was more than happy to evolve into a "yes" horse if he liked what he saw in his handler. Although I herded him around the round pen that day, it was he who gave me the perfect push of inspiration and motivation in my heart and soul. That black stallion was like an angel to me. His presence and wonderful attitude kept me from giving up when I was at my lowest of lows. He brought me back to the wonderful world of horses, and it wasn't very long before my frame of mind got back to normal, too. After all, I had a business to run, a family to support, and that meant engagements to keep. But the pounding my spirit took at the fury of that big, blood-red mare stuck with me for months. I couldn't seem to let it go. What had happened between Stella and me? Where did that violence come from? Was it justified? Did I do the right thing, or did I just lose control and beat on a horse?

They say that confusion and conflict are signs of growth waiting to happen. Well, I had plenty of both. Growth wasn't coming easy, and that old saying wasn't bringing me any comfort at all. I could sense I was wrestling with something important and that the struggle would be worth it. But I wasn't getting anywhere with it. Somewhere deep inside me, I could almost hear a demonic cackle.

I was trying to resolve a paradox.

Like the age-old question of whether it's best to give "an eye for an eye" or "turn the other cheek," or whether it was better for the well-being of my children to stay in my marriage with Anita or end it, I knew that on the one hand something had to be done with Stella. She was a danger to herself and others and to let her continue on the way she was would simply have been another form of abuse, like a doctor withholding a medicine that he knows would relieve his patient's suffering. Just calming Stella down and then walking away from her wasn't an option. It would have violated everything I've tried to live by for the last decade. I had to do something.

On the other hand, what did I actually do? One thing was for sure: I'd beaten the aggressive and threatening pushiness out of that horse pretty good. But I was afraid I'd been guilty of something much more than just abusing a horse—bad as that is. I was afraid I'd been guilty of a colossal collapse of integrity. I'd promised Stella compassion and healing and security; instead, she got violence and intimidation. I'd spent my whole life fighting against that kind of behavior, yet somehow the blackness seemed to have ridden over me. And the guilt didn't stop there. That audience had come to me in the belief that I'd show them how to deal with their horses more compassionately. If I betrayed Stella, I betrayed them as well. I had become one more so-called leader who couldn't walk the talk, just like the lying politicians and preachers and incompetent bosses they dealt with every day. I had promised them so much more. And I had failed miserably.

On the one hand, the people in that demonstration were looking to me for leadership and damn it, I had led. On the other hand, the way I had gone about it seemed to undercut everything I've professed to stand for. I wondered if I was the horse world's answer to that U.S. military commander in Vietnam who justified the smoking ruins he left behind him by saying: "To save the village, we had to destroy it."

It all seemed to revolve around the anger I'd felt. It wasn't that I had been blinded by anger—it was more like being ablaze with it. I'd needed that rage. It was what gave me the courage and strength to go toe to toe with Stella in order to start her journey out of her torment. I guess you could call it tough love. But at the same time, I—and quite a few others—had been sickened by the wreckage and violence my anger had left in its wake. In the name of defending myself, I had struck that horse again and again until I left her body marked with welts. I needed the anger to accomplish my goal, to give me the strength I needed to accept the responsibility that had been thrust on me—responsibility that, to be honest, I had sought. But how I used my rage shredded the spirit of what I was hoping to achieve. At some point that afternoon, I was afraid I had passed over the razor-thin edge from healer and teacher to whip-cracking conqueror.

The longer I thought about the problem, the more it seemed to boil down to this: in order to accomplish what I thought I had to accomplish with Stella, I had had to tap into parts of myself that I had avoided for years—for almost as long as I had known of their existence. Pride and anger were hallmarks of a side of my psyche that had caused me so many problems in the past. They'd caused hurt and anguish for others, too. I had wanted nothing to do with them and I'd spent years running from those old enemies, ever since the morning in the monastery chapel when I'd come face to face with the demon that lived inside me. I'd tried pretending it wasn't there and all that happened was addiction, dysfunction, and pain. Then I'd tried discipline. If I couldn't pretend there was no problem, then I would hobble the beast and lead it out of the arena to hide it where people could never see it. I'd lock my shadow away in a dark stable deep inside of me. That worked for a while, and yet here it was, free of its chains, rearing its ugly head and prancing in front of me. Even worse, I had been forced to turn to this shameful secret self for help.

When I faced this truth, something in me cracked. And through that crack a ray of light began to shine.

Since the turn of the last century, we've grown accustomed to thinking of our psyches as being divided in two, the conscious and the unconscious mind. Different thinkers have put different spins on that polarity. Sigmund Freud called the two halves the ego and the id. The ego was the seat of the intellect, the home of rationality. In the id roiled our untamed passions, sexual drives, and emotions. Freud's colleague and rival Carl Jung analyzed the split a bit differently. He and Freud were pretty much sitting on the same analyst's couch when it came to the nature and function of the conscious mind. But in the unconscious, Jung saw a stew of archetypes—a series of highly charged images whose patterns and symbolic meanings guided all forms of human behavior. What's more, archetypes were pretty much the same the world over. They took slightly different forms in different cultures, but they had much more in common. Like different creeks and rivers all spilling into the same ocean, the fact that we all share these unconscious symbols links our minds on a deep level. Jung called this shared psychic ocean in which we all mentally and emotionally swim together the collective unconscious.

Now, far be it for me to try to overturn more than a century of psychological thought, but as I meditated on what had happened to me with Stella it occurred to me that there might be a third way to understand the conscious/unconscious polarity. Think about it. On one side there's rationality, logic, and the individual "I." On the other, there's instinct, emotion, and collectivity. Suggest anything?

By this point, it should. We're right back full circle to talking about predator and prey.

Our conscious mind takes us out and about in the world. This is the mind that plans, that sets goals, that achieves. Our unconscious mind, on the other hand, stays in the dark, hiding like a rabbit. It's full of urges and drives—not specific goals, but raw, undirected energy akin to the unfocused awareness of a horse. It's in the nature of the conscious mind—the ego, as Freud would say—to want to take over and control the whole show. After all, control is what predators do. The ego takes all our repressed fears, our desires, our anger and denial—everything that doesn't play by its rules—shoves them down into the subconscious and ties them up tight to the hitching post where they can't get out. Eventually, this restrained subconscious becomes almost a mirror image of our ego, the face we present to the world. It becomes our Shadow self. It's full of everything our conscious mind doesn't want to acknowledge—not only the fear and denial, but our compulsions, our hidden dreams, our obsessions, and our drives. Anything that threatens to upset the equanimity the ego seeks to present to the world gets stuffed down into our Shadows. We treat our Shadows a lot like we treat our horses: we lock them up and try to control them. I'd been doing that to my Shadow for decades.

The more I thought about this new way to understand what had happened to me, the wider the opening in that light-filled crack grew.

So many of us treat our Shadow selves like a horse that everyone says is bad. We restrain it and lock it away, and the more we fear our Shadow the tighter we hold the reins with which we attempt to control ourselves. But what our Shadows need isn't more restraints and hobbles, but healing and understanding. Like a horse, our Shadows need fresh air and movement. They don't need domineering dictators, they need partners who will give them boundaries yet let them run. How would we treat a horse that's rebellious, angry, even dangerous? We'd take her into the round pen. We'd try to harness that energy without destroying it by making her move in a way that's natural to her, and then showing her that she can comfortably accept that that movement would only be shepherded with boundaries of where not to go. Sooner or later, with correct alignment, consistent motivation, the conviction of our boundaries, and all the other spokes branching out from the hub of the wheel of shepherding the prey, even the most difficult horses find themselves relieved and more comfortable as they find the leader that can offer them the perfect push.

Similarly, we need to take our Shadows into a mental round pen— not to let them rage uncontrolled, but to learn how to work with them instead of denying them.

After all, the predator/prey model tells us that the two halves of such a polarity need each other. They are symbiotic, and if one side falls out of balance or becomes too powerful, both sides suffer eventually. If wolves don't cull the deer herds, there's mass starvation in the winter as too many deer strip the meadows of grass. And if there are too many wolves, they deplete the resources their long-term survival depends on. In short, we need to integrate both halves of our personality. Just as we must balance the predator/prey dynamic in the round pen, we must do it in our own minds. The daunting challenge is that we live in such a dog-eat-dog predatory world that we feel our weaknesses and vulnerabilities are best kept hidden away from probable attack. I began to look at my Shadow, not as something to be denied, but as something that needed training and healing so that it could be fully incorporated, at last, into my life.

We can't ignore our ego. It allows us to make rational choices, to understand the world and make reasoned decisions in it. It sets our goals and gives us the discipline to achieve them. It pushes us into the world and gives us the ability to take control of our lives. But we can be so much more if we can balance those attributes with those of our

Shadow side. The Shadow is a source of energy and passion. It allows us to follow our instincts. It gives us inspiration. And yes, it can give our will the unbridled force it sometimes needs. Sometimes we do need to go to war, and the Shadow feeds our warrior spirit.

The crack had swung wide open. Blinking in the sudden bright, I smiled at how obvious it should have been. The horses had been trying to tell me this all along.

We've already talked about how horses mirror back to us what's really going on in our hearts. The horses see our Shadow and react to it all the time. We can see the outline it leaves on their bodies. They'll tell us exactly who we hope we aren't, if we know how to listen. Every horse I'd worked with in every round pen I'd entered had been telling me about my Shadow. I thought I'd thoroughly stuffed it away, but it was, and always has been, written all over my body. I'd learned to speak the body language of horses with reasonable fluency, but I never lost my Shadow accent. If I'd been aware enough and focused enough on what the horses had been telling me right from the start, I would have been given this great gift of self-awareness a long time ago.

You see, I believe that those archetypes that Jung wrote about are real. I believe they do live inside us and have power that we can harness. One of those archetypes is the horse, and it is a particularly powerful archetype. The horse evokes feelings that encompass power, freedom, sexuality, and danger. For many Native American tribes the totem of the horse signified the balanced use or abuse of power. And for Jung, the horse didn't represent one particular event or character. The meaning of the horse archetype was constantly shifting. Sometimes it stood for the Child archetype, sometimes it was the Great Mother, sometimes it was the Wise Old Man. Just look at how prevalent the image of the horse is as a logo or marketing tool in our culture and it's clear that the Horse archetype touches many sides of us.

I don't pretend to understand intellectually how this process works. But I've felt it in myself and seen it in others and I'm convinced it's real. When we work with a horse, we have a thousand pounds of living, breathing archetype prancing around in front of us or underneath us. When we are with the horses, the object of our focused attention in the physical world corresponds exactly to a series of crucial images and symbolic meanings in our inner world. That correspondence stirs up something inside us, and the better we get at balancing focus with awareness the more profound is that stirring. Somewhere, that stirring around of the parts of our deepest selves gives us a chance to learn about it and work with it. I don't have any scientific way of describing this process, but it's there.

All I can do is draw comparisons. We can think of the collective unconscious as being like the Internet—a vast, invisible network of interlinked images, arguments, information, and stories. Horses function like a high-speed cable connection, allowing us access to this seemingly infinite storehouse of information. Our Shadow self is stabled in this storehouse. That makes working with horses one of the best ways to reach it, work with it, and understand it. Horses can be a form of active meditation that teaches us to find balance between our two sides—predator and prey, conscious and unconscious—as we learn to synthesize body, mind, and spirit through nonvictimizing competition. The martial artists call it satori: when body, mind, and spirit are all working together as one, fully aware and in the moment, poised, ready, willing, and able to perform at maximum competitive potential.

This, I believe, is the final step we must take in order to earn the right to leadership of our horses or with each other. I've written before about the importance of consistency. Consistency, I am convinced, equals integrity. And without integrity, there is only betrayal and dysfunction. If you don't walk the talk, you're just another authority figure spreading waves of disappointment and disillusion in your wake. We see all around the corrosive effects of that kind of fake leadership: cynicism, apathy, and an ethical bar that gets lower with every news cycle. We don't want to be part of that, not on any level. Our families, our employees, the kids we coach in Little League and the friends who value our opinion both want and need more from us.

We can't be consistent, however, until we learn to balance our conscious self and our Shadow self. Until we achieve that, our Shadow self, like a horse pacing in its stall, will continue to feel wound up tighter and tighter until it suddenly springs up like a jack-in-the-box and knocks us off the rails time and again, as so often happened with me. We just won't be fully in command of ourselves. We will sabotage ourselves over and over. We'll be having affairs in the White House; we'll be rationalizing illegal wars; we'll be coming up with terms like "aggressive accounting" to cover up our thievery. We will, inevitably, let down ourselves and everyone who ever had faith in us.

This is the meaning of Socrates' command to "know thyself": to know not only the good and the bad we're capable of, but also how the good and the bad within us are intertwined. It's only when our two selves are working together that we can be truly consistent. There will be no surprises. Horses—and people—will be able to count on us 100 percent of the time.

Don't get me wrong, though. Consistency doesn't mean that we need to be obsessive and work at training our horses, or our kids, or our employees, all day, every day. It's not really about quantity of time; it's about quality of time. I have seen so many people who train their horses on average for two hours a day, six days a week, but because they are inconsistent in how they act and react while they are with their horses they never seem to make any progress. On the other hand, if you only get to your horse two or three times per week, perhaps for only thirty or forty minutes per session, but while you're there with them they can predict with 100 percent accuracy how you will behave and they know that your behavior is truly in their best interests, their willingness and performance will continue to get better and better.

Consistency also does not need to be rigid or inflexible. We've been talking about a balance of two sides, not a domination of one by the other. And a balance is always dynamic. It may look motionless, but a constant shift and flow maintains that stillness. As always, I look to nature. Populations of predators and prey shift from year to year, with the foxes thriving one season and the rabbits the next. But over the long term, they stay within balance.

I meditate regularly. Not only has it become the cornerstone of how I feed my spirit, it's also where I turn for insight into questions that trouble me. For me, the goal of meditation isn't always to clear my mind. Most often, I just let my thoughts go wherever they want like horses turned out on the prairie. I was doing that one morning, deep into meditation, when an image came into my head of two doors. One was black, one was white. A deep, booming voice ordered: "Choose!" I hung there, paralyzed by the choice, not willing to forsake either one of the doors for the other. Finally, my heart must have convinced my ego to just let go of the stress of needing to choose, and I felt the trepidation melt away as I heard my voice gently say, "No." The two doors began to tremble, then they moved together and merged into a single door colored many shades of gray. The door swung wide open; and in my vision, or whatever it was, I walked through it and as I did I heard my inner voice softly say, "The answer is... it depends." I had to laugh. This was literally an "inside" joke that I had played upon myself. Don't get me wrong. By seeing things in shades of gray I am not talking about living a life of mediocrity. Far from it.

This happens all the time in my clinics: Someone will describe a problem they're trying to resolve and ask me what I would do. They think they are asking a short question and are looking for a quick and easy fix or trick or gimmick for an answer. Almost always, I answer, "It depends." Why their horse is bucking, or rearing, or too fast, or too slow, or running away from jumps, or refusing to load in the trailer; why they can't get the right lead, or any of the thousands of questions that people have about not being able to get what they want from their horses, is always subject to too many variables, too many areas of cause and effect between people and horses, predator and prey. The answers these people are looking for can't be found without being able to see the issues in their entirety and then by addressing them at the most basic level of cause.

This is why, if you've been reading this book looking for a series of handy-dandy solutions to the problems you may be having with your horse, you're probably about ready to throw my story at the wall. I can't give you such a list because there isn't one. In every case, there are many factors that have to go into the balance before any kind of decision can be made.

I believe something in my Shadow self was trying to teach me a lesson about leadership and balance. Wise leaders learn to avoid black-and-white extremes. Extremes are never in balance. And because they are unbalanced, extremes can only be maintained through coercion. Coercion is what I resorted to with Stella and subsequently she became the catalyst for this entire book on learning how to avoid it. It doesn't help anyone, human or horse. And in the end, it corrodes the spirit of the person doing the coercing. A balanced leader will look for balanced solutions.

I don't have a dogma for dealing with specific issues. I'm not being wish-washy. It's just being balanced and realistic. After all, we're talking about finding answers to problems as we move from being inconsistent, reactive predators who cover symptoms with Band-Aids to becoming consistent, proactive, predator/prey-balanced beings who see straight into root causes. Why can't you catch your horse? Well, that depends. Why do you think your horse should want you to catch her?

Of course, sometimes the middle way between two extremes is the toughest position of all. You're an easy target from both sides when trying to walk a tightrope between them. Horses can help you here, too. If we learn the lessons of self-awareness they're trying to teach us, we will reach decisions and choose paths that are rooted in the wisdom of both sides of our personality. That will give us conviction. And if we have that solidly rooted conviction, we will find the courage we need to stick to them. Let me tell you about a dream I had not too long ago.

I was in the middle of a straight-and-narrow prairie road. There were two of us, both my light and dark sides, and we were debating where to place a beautiful throne we had with us. We were taking ourselves very seriously. We decided that the only "balanced" place for the throne was in the middle of the road. Just then a big truck came along and drove right over my gorgeous throne, crushing it. "Get his license plate number!" I cried out, but the truck was going too fast and there was too much dust to see clearly. I was upset, ranting about the fact that the chair cost me a pretty penny. And that's the second time this had happened to me. A previous throne had apparently been flattened by a vehicle coming from the other direction.

When I woke up, I began to meditate. As soon as I felt I was centered and balanced, I asked my unconscious, my Shadow, for an answer to this strange dream. Suddenly, I began to laugh.

I realized that in my quest for balance and unity I automatically assumed that I needed to be in the middle of the road. Of course, when you do that, you get run over from both sides! My meditation showed me the image of a stone bridge going over the road, with a new chair sitting perfectly balanced on top of the arch. Not to the left, not to the right, not in the way in the middle, simply above. Then I asked, "What do I make my bridges out of?" and suddenly the bridge turned into a rainbow. I knew then that the rainbow represented my own personal energies and choices, causes and effects. I knew then when I needed to make a decision, either an easy or serious one, as long as I was coming from the center of my unified self I would always make the appropriate choice. Only when we are truly centered and balanced and unified between the light and the dark sides of our nature can we rise above the limitations of polarity.

In the meditation on the road I found the serenity to accept what is and allowed the road to be and I simply built my bridge above. The choice between knowing when to serenely accept or when to coura-geously change requires wisdom, and wisdom can only be found after a critical mass of experience has taught us to always stay centered in our unified beings and not fall over to one polarity or the other.

Horses can provide that experience. Bonding with horses can be an active meditation of the body, mind, and spirit working to find balance between opposites, predator and prey. This experience or way of being is so balanced it opens the gateway to finding balance within us.

This, finally, was what I learned from Stella. Until I met her, I was living and working under the assumption, conscious or not, that my Shadow could be ignored as if it didn't exist. And if I couldn't ignore it, I would simply discipline it back into submission. Stella forced me to admit not only that my Shadow existed—the welts on her were proof enough of that—but that sometimes I needed it. Sometimes, I needed the strength and energy that anger and pride could give me. Sometimes, instinct was the only pilot that could see me through. Sometimes, I had to lose control to gain control.

I opened this book with the image of a dark horse, bearing down on me out of the shadows. It's an image familiar to many of us from the Book of Revelation as the third horse of the apocalypse, the dark horse that brings famine and devastation. This book has nothing to do with famine, but I borrowed that image for a reason. For most of my life, my Shadow has lived inside me like a dark horse, and when-ever I felt it stir and kick, my reaction was fear and control. No, I didn't think a judgmental God was angry with us and that the world was going to end—but I was afraid of my own personal meltdown, the final struggle between the face I presented to the world and my Shadow self. And perhaps my greatest hidden fear of all was how vul-nerable, unworthy, and angry I really felt about my ability to main-tain a positive and optimistic attitude in life while living in the shad-ow of a Creator who has apparently set us up to learn the hardest les-son of all—how to find our balance and inner peace as we strive for-ward in a world full of paradox.

I smile now at that fear. In the Bible, the third horse of the apocalypse is ridden by a man carrying a set of scales. As I thought about it,
I realized that the dark horse was bringing balance, not strife. I realized it was coming to cooperate, not annihilate. That horse, in the
physical form of Stella, was coming to join with me and move together in concert. Thank God, I finally figured that out. I've been dancing
with the dark horse ever since.

[13]

happy trails

I MEET A LOT of people as I travel from horse show to clinic to workshop, and it's gratifying to realize how many of those people have read my first book, *Horses Don't Lie*. Quite a few of those people have questions arising from that book, and one of the most common ones is: How's Etiquette?

Etiquette was a horse I used to own, a big aggressive Dutch Warmblood, 16.2 hands high. I met Etiquette when his then-owner, the renowned dressage trainer Willy Arts, invited me to see if I could start him. Etiquette had been intended to be the foundation sire of an Olympic-class breeding program, and he was quite a horse—powerful, macho, and loaded with presence. He hadn't got off to a good start with the people Willy had bought him from, however, and he was explosive with anger and could be downright vicious. But during a wildly athletic round-pen session, he and I bonded on the very first day. When I finally swung up onto his back, I felt the most powerful surge of waves I'd ever experienced on a horse. On Etiquette, I was definitely surfing the big one! And more than that, Etiquette and I connected in a deeper way than I'd ever felt before. This was not another T.C. Etiquette was an adamant "no" horse who became a "maybe" horse and then went all the way and was transformed into a "yes" horse in a very big way. As we worked together, I felt that horse completely surrender his mind, body, and spirit to me without giving up a bit of that powerful equine machismo that made him so special. He was an amazing horse, the kind of horse you want to ride for the rest of your life.

But when Anita and I made the decision to return to Canada, we knew we'd need capital to get us going. Etiquette was by far our most valuable asset, and we had to put him up for sale. I'd bought and sold hundreds of horses by then and had long ago given up on sentimentality, but watching Etiquette walk into someone else's trailer was hard. Very, very hard. But, like any responsible parent needing to provide for his or her family, I did what I had to do.

So how's Etiquette? He's fine. He's getting well into the twilight of his career, but the woman I sold him to treated him well and he had many great years roaming and riding over the high Nevada desert. He's now retired, as happy and mellow a horse as I've ever met. Etiquette, once so fierce that the grooms had to feed him by tossing hay into his stall and then running for their lives, is now regularly turned out with the herd. He's one of the guys.

I kept in touch with Etiquette because he was the last horse I owned for years. I sold him in 1995. It was seven years before I owned another horse.

I'm not sure why. It just never worked out, just as Anita's and my plans for a horse training institute had never worked out. Just like, I suppose, Anita and I hadn't worked out. It's not as if I haven't had horses to ride. I've been fortunate to work with some pretty high-end stables, and I've had plenty of half-million dollar horses underneath my breeches. But those seven years without my own horse were turbulent ones for me, both in my business and in my personal life. It takes time and energy to replace a horse like Etiquette and with a family, and a business that kept me out on the road, I didn't have enough of either.

I missed that kind of connection, though—missed it badly. As my marriage slowly crumbled and the pressures of my growing business increased, I felt increasingly drained in every way. I was constantly giving out but there was nothing coming in to replenish my reserves. I was becoming more and more burned out.

I finally realized how bad it was getting one afternoon in a riding arena where I was giving a workshop. As I was putting the first ride on a wonderful "yes" horse, a big, bold, Swedish Warmblood mare, for the first time in years, I felt something like the connection I had experienced with my old friend Etiquette. It was like coming home. It was like falling in love. It was like meeting a friend I hadn't seen in years. It was overwhelming, and I just fell apart. All my frustrations over my relationships, all my guilt over not being at home enough for my kids and all my soul-deep fatigue bubbled over. When I got off that horse, I buried my head in her big, muscular shoulder, and in front of two hundred and fifty people, I wept. After that, I knew I needed to find a horse I could call my own.

Kathryn and I started looking around, and once word spread we got offered a lot of nice horses. Nothing clicked with me, however, until months later. We were on the road we got a call from a friend in Toronto. She wanted to tell us about an absolute monster of a horse she had just seen at a nearby facility, a Hanoverian mare, 17.2 hands high, with enough of the finest European bloodlines to be in an Olympic training program. Kathryn and I were scheduled to be in the area soon, so a few days later we dropped in to take a look.

By that time, I'd started having dreams about a horse—a big, black mare, both athletic and elegant, rearing up into the air, twirling her head in anger and striking the ground in frustration. I've had so many mystical experiences in my life that by now I was not the least bit surprised when I walked into the barn and saw the mare of my dreams, the nightmare in the flesh. I didn't have to be told which one was the horse we'd come to see. I knew. She knew, too. She fixed her eyes on me the moment I walked in to the stables and didn't take them off me the whole time I was there. I knew this was my horse, but I didn't say anything to Kathryn because I couldn't afford her. She was as much as the deposit on a house. But Kathryn, always one step ahead of me, figured me out anyway. She bought me that magnificent animal for Christmas. On Christmas Day, I was already out playing with my new horse.

The first thing I did was to change her name. I called her "Tsunami," after the Japanese word for tidal wave, because I could feel she would come to symbolize a wave of massive change in my life. I was right. (Please know that I named her two years before the unprecedented killer tsunami that struck Asia on December 26, 2004, and that her name is not meant to be heartless or in poor taste.)

I began the journey that resulted in this book from a place of isolation and disarray. All my most important alignments—with my wife and with my children—were either over or were in flux. Of course, I stayed in regular contact with Anita and our two children, but after Anita and I split up there wasn't really anyplace I could call home—anyplace that didn't have wheels under it, anyway. I was spending too much time on the road and not nearly enough with Raven and Adler. I was rapidly burning myself out, and I didn't seem to be getting any nearer to my lifelong dream of a horse institute. It was, quite frankly, lonely and disheartening. I felt that I was going backward, regressing to the days after I left the monastery when I traveled around in my camper truck with only my late, lamented dog Dudley for company. Here I go again, I thought, only this time my dog is named Farley. When am I ever going to learn.

I was being a little too hard on myself. I was afraid that I was just circling around, going back over the same old ground, but I wasn't. I wasn't doing that at all. In an earlier chapter, we talked about the idea of a spiral path. Look at a spiral from the top and you see an endlessly repeating circle. Look at it from the side and you see constant ascension. When I look back at things now, I believe that side view represents what I've truly been doing.

Chris riding Tsunami.

In the end, it was all a question of timing—and alignment. I wasn't correctly aligned. And the time wasn't right. Those are two of the most basic concepts I teach, but I had to go back again and get them right. No quality forward is possible unless alignment, then timing, is correct.

To get things right, I had to return to some first principles that I've sworn by ever since I was that serious, questing young man who first set out on the road. As long ago as back then, I promised myself that I would passionately love the woman I was with, or I wouldn't be with her. I swore I would never waste my life doing a job I didn't care intensely about. And I vowed that I would remain rootless until I found my spiritual home. I was not about to, as Thoreau said, lead a life "of quiet desperation." Those may not be your rules of alignment, but they're mine. And I now know, at the age of forty-four, after four marriages, two countries, hundreds of riding stables, and uncounted thousands of miles on the road, that I have finally satisfied them.

Meeting Kathryn had changed everything for me. What used to be so difficult was now so much easier. And my kids love her. In fact, Raven and Adler performed a special wedding ceremony for us where they officially presided over our union and gave us their blessings. I'm not saying that any of this was easy for any of us. But my kids, coming into ages eleven and nine, are now very clear and comfortable with the fact that their parents are genuinely happier and easier to live with in the company of their new mates.

Anita has also found herself moving forward with a new career in radio broadcasting and a new relationship with a great guy by the name of Everett. My kids will be the first to tell you that they did not lose a father when Anita and I divorced; they gained two great new parents in Kathryn and Everett. Now, when we all get together for special occasions, we are a level-headed herd that brings out the best in each other. Another example, I think, of alignment and the need to give up control in order to gain control.

My new home—my first home, really—is in the northern

foothills of Alberta's Rocky Mountains and I found it exactly one year to the day after my life-changing encounter with Stella. There's a song that talks about "coming home to a place he'd never been before," and that's how it felt the first time I walked on to this land. These foothills are a special place. They're one of the few places left on the continent where the rugged wilderness, flowery meadows, and the clear, rushing rivers aren't clotted with resorts, condo developments, or vacation homes. It's here in Alberta that I'm finally settling down to build the institute I've dreamed of for so long. Riversong Ranch Equestrian Retreat is the name we have given our new property, and the blue-green glacier-fed waters of the McLeod River are always there as a constant reminder of one of the cornerstone metaphors of my teaching. The expansive river flows level and strong through our land, channeled by the grassy riverbanks, and I'm finally feeling that way again myself. This, I feel in the very marrow of my bones, is where the universe wants me to be. This is where I'll be able to most clearly hear everything Nature is trying to tell me. These mystical forests of pristine wilderness overflowing with deer, elk, hawks, eagles, cougar, and bear is where I'll be able to follow the horses and the abundant wildlife around me ever deeper into the collective unconscious that guides all our best thoughts and decisions.

That, I believe, is going to lie at the heart of this next cycle I've started: learning to hear that small voice that speaks quietly and clearly within us all. I know it's there. I've heard it—or rather, it's heard me. Let me tell you one last story about one last horse. His name is Peek-a-Boo.

Back in 1995, when Anita and I moved back to Canada from Nevada in hopes of reinventing ourselves in the country of our birth, we brought along with us a couple of our favorite horses. One of them was a wild horse, a solid black mustang I had adopted that Raven aptly named Peek-a-Boo. Peek-a-Boo was a true wild mustang, with about the same relationship to a domestic horse as a coyote or a wolf has to a golden retriever. Like the wild animal he was, he always kept to the shadows and hid as much as possible. And because this little black mustang would always hide behind other horses, a barn wall, or whatever he could find to avoid being caught, Raven called him Peek-a-Boo. There he'd be, trying to be invisible, with his little black nose poking around the corner of the hay shed. Raven would sing out, "Peek-a-Boo, I see you," and then we'd have to go catch him. He never once willingly walked up to any human being and he never, ever bowed his head long and low to the ground. I was able to get him started under saddle easily enough but he never liked it. He was always stoic and reserved.

This went on for years with Peek-a-Boo until one year I was invited to present a clinic at a horse exposition in Louisville, Kentucky, called Equitana. It's one of the biggest in the world and I was thrilled to be asked. I would be with the biggest names in this business, and I knew, as the new kid on the block, that I'd have to do something special to get some attention. So I asked the show organizers for the most challenging and aggressive horse they could find. It's relatively easy, if you know how, to gain the trust of a horse that's merely skittish, and the audience eats it up as much as if the horse were truly difficult. But nobody was dealing with the equine bullies that are so common in the real world. These days there are just as many horses abusing people as there are people abusing horses, and none of my colleagues seemed to want to go there. So for my four days at Equitana I wanted the baddest, most difficult horse they could find in Kentucky. And I got him.

He was a three-year-old Morgan stallion named Gus, yet another black horse. Gus was a mayhem machine. He needed to be led around with a stud chain over his nose and often in his mouth. His owners were incredibly patient but they were at their wits' end as to how to get anywhere with their very delinquent young stallion. It took three people to lead him into the round pen where I was waiting. And when they finally took the chains off him, Gus exploded. He bucked, reared, struck, and kicked out in all directions. Then he started galloping around the round pen throwing every nasty gesture a horse can express into the center of the circle, directed clearly at me. I was impressed and a little in awe. Gus wasn't big, perhaps only 15.1 hands, but he had enough spirit for two or three horses his size.

So I went to work with the little black dynamo, and we had a great time together. Gus dodged in and out at me, throwing kicks, bucking, twirling his head in anger, and striking at me, but all while he kept moving forward. Even when he'd rear up and get all full of himself, it was easy to send a little push with a gentle flick of the whip at his shoulder and back down to earth he'd come, galloping off in a new direction, but nonetheless yielding to my push. Usually, audiences at events like these expect to see a horse not only gentled, but bridled, saddled, and ridden within a one-hour session. Gus had a lot further to go than most of the horses people work with, and I thought it was enough for the first day that he had lost his frustration and anger and had been transformed into a little boy scout. Like my old friend Etiquette, Gus was still as macho as ever but now he was controlling it. That was a good note on which to end our first time together and tomorrow would be another day. The audience appeared to genuinely appreciate my detailed explanations, not only of what I did do, but what I refused to do.

When Gus and I got together again the next day, the size of the crowd had doubled. Again, Gus came in more like a lion than a lamb, but this time it took me only about ten minutes before we were right back where we left off. Then I worked him "in hand," with the halter on the end of the lunge line. I used my contact to mesmerize him with focus and calm his nerves with endorphins. We made huge progress for another hour, but again, I still had not even saddled this horse, let alone mounted him. Still, the applause from the audience suggested they understood that just because we could get on a horse for a first ride that doesn't necessarily mean that we should.

By day three, the stands were full as an even larger crowd gathered to see what would happen next. Gus came in full of himself but settled into the work very quickly and began indicating with his body language that he was now ready to consider a saddle and bridle. By the end of that session Gus was carrying himself proudly round and collected as he danced in front of the audience wearing a saddle and bridle for the first time. He was truly close, very close to being ready for his first ride and I thought for sure that during our one hour session the next day, our last together, Gus would let me mount up and ride his waves.

On day four you couldn't find a seat in the grandstand, and everyone was waiting to see if I would climb aboard Gus. All of the other clinicians were already riding their horses—although I have to say that I saw far more force with relatively easy horses than finesse with truly hard horses. And I saw a lot of miserable, unbalanced horses. I wanted to prove that a horse, any horse, could end up being a happy and beautifully balanced mover if the rider really knew how to read all of the horse signals and worked with the horse's agenda instead of his own.

Before trying to ride Gus, I began to long line or "drive" him. The ground driving was awesome and Gus traveled around that pen like a third-level dressage horse. But when it was time for me to try to mount him for the first time, Gus wasn't having it. I know how to ease myself up into the tack for the first time, and this stallion wanted nothing to do with it. He started rearing and let out a huge buck whenever I even thought about putting the slightest weight into the stirrup. He was letting everybody know that, in his mind, it was he who was supposed to be doing the mounting of other creatures, namely mares, and he wanted nothing to do with his new leader assuming that it was okay to climb on top of him. I pushed and herded him from the ground into some difficult gymnastic movements. I was herding him into hard work, which he could understand as a consequence for his challenging me.

Before long Gus was very close to letting me climb aboard. His tail was now calm and curled instead of swishing with annoyance and the

pushing into gymnastic exercises had left him level-headed and licking his lips. He wasn't humping up and pinning his ears back as I put
weight in the stirrup. Now it was time to ride—except for one small
problem. I only had a few short minutes left and at these shows when
you are out of time you are out of the arena.

Gus was almost there but I had a decision to make. I stood next to
Gus as if ready to climb aboard, left it all behind and went within and
tried to center myself. I asked myself what I should do. I knew I could
most likely ride through any residual rear, buck, or bolt that might
still flare up. But I didn't want to have to do that. I'm always saying to
my students, and I had said it time and again to the Equitana audience, a good cowboy can ride a bucking horse but a great rider's horse
doesn't need to buck. I did not want Gus's first ride to be forced. I felt
I owed him that. I would probably have taken another fifteen minutes
to get Gus totally ready, but that was fifteen more minutes than I had.
So when I went within and asked myself, and Gus, what to do. The
answer I got was, "Let it be and walk away."

When I explained to the audience why I wasn't going to mount up
on Gus, they gave me a standing ovation. They clearly got the message
that it was in Gus's best interests—and also in the best interests of his
owners—for his first ride to be nonstressful instead of forced. It was
so obvious that he was very close and everybody knew it wasn't going
to take much more. After all the smoke and mirrors I'd been seeing in
round pen demonstrations, the audience's approval was far more gratifying than the ride would have been.

But what about Peek-a-Boo? Well, I returned home from that
show beaming, calm, and confident for the first time over my future
in this business. And when I got home one of the first things I did was
to go out back of the barn to check on my horses that had been turned
out in pasture while I was away. The herd was way out back, literally
in the south forty, and as I began the long walk toward them I saw one
horse leave the herd and start walking directly toward me. I couldn't
believe my eyes; it was Peek-a-Boo. I stopped in my tracks and that

..... black mustang just kept coming. He walked right up to me, stood in front of me, and bowed. And he bowed again and again, dipping his head low, raising it to level and then dipping it low again. He had the softest, sweetest look in his eyes instead of the usual hard glare of stoic defiance, and at that moment every cell in my body began to tingle and the chills ran up and down my spine. I began to cry with tears of joy and wonder. Somehow, Peek-a-Boo knew what had happened in Kentucky. And Peek-a-Boo was letting me know that I had passed his test. He was bowing to me because of how I handled the situation with Gus. Peek-a-Boo was speaking to me from the collective unconscious, and since that day I've never looked at anybody or anything with the same sense of distance and isolation I used to feel. I know now that deep down inside we all are the same, we do all come from the same source and we can all know whatever we need to know, hear whatever it is we need to hear, if we just learn how to listen. It's just that so many of us human beings have buried our connection to knowingness so deep within the same dungeon where we hold our inner horses prisoner that we only really hear it through the distorted and murky waters of our dreams. Our Shadows live in the collective unconscious, and our Shadows know.

I know that even as I work at listening to that shadowy voice, I'll have to circle back again and work on basic concepts. But I now understand that every time I do, I'll be working on a higher level. And if I listen closely enough, that shadowy voice will help me through.

This is what I hope for my students, as well. We'll never perfect the basics. We'll be working on alignment, forward, contact, timing, level, bend, boundaries, and collection for as long as we ride—or as long as we care about the quality of our lives. We'll always be working on the balance between our outward selves and our Shadow selves, too. Sometimes, it'll probably feel like you're making the same mistakes over and over again. Remember to tell yourself that you're not. You're making mistakes, sure, but they're better mistakes. You're screwing up on a higher level. Cold comfort, maybe, but it's the way

ANITA IRWIN

As Chris leads in six of his horses from the pasture, the herd sees a camera lens aimed directly at them. This focused intent from the camera suggests to the horses the "hard prowling stare" of a predator. Peek-a-boo, the black wild mustang, decides to try and avoid the camera by hiding behind Chris.

we move forward. We can let it first change ourselves, then ripple out from us into our relationship with the world. If we're in a position of leadership—and almost all of us find ourselves there somewhere along the road—we can create a space around us where that principle can thrive. Others will learn, and the world, very slowly, might even start to change.

Frankly, I think this world could use a little transformational change and I think I can see the ripples beginning to spread. Students at my workshops take these ideas and start to teach them to others. Now I find myself working with psychologists, psychiatrists, mental health workers, and therapists of all kinds, and more and more of them are learning how to work with horses in order to heal themselves. This work in equine-assisted personal development, or EAPD, is focused on leaders working with the horses in order to learn from

Chris and Kathryn swimming with a dolphin while in Bermuda on their honeymoon.

the experience of the eightfold path of horse sense. The goal is always to improve their self-awareness and balance so that they develop enhanced insights and skills in how they go about working with the people in their lives whom they hope to help further along on their journey inwards to reach and heal their Shadows. And the horses always help us reach our goals

It's easy to be cynical about the direction our world is going. You can list the world's problems as easily as I can. But I know there are thousands of people out there looking for better ways to align themselves in it. They'll find it, and they'll start to move forward. They'll meet the dark horse and learn to dance with it. The rhythm of those hoofbeats will draw others in, and together, maybe, someday we'll ride

level-headed and collected into a sunny meadow where
ance of our Shadows is welcomed, not feared.

AND IT WON'T just be our horses and our Shadows that we've
learned to listen to. The horses can show us how to balance our predator ego nature with our prey inner self so that we can learn how to
evolve out of polarity into a truly unified way of being that allows us
to be at peace within ourselves. A unified being is, as corny as it
sounds, "at one" with itself and this is the path to spiritual enlightenment.. But aside from the horses, the "winds of change" will always
blow, sometimes as a gentle breeze and sometimes like a tornado, to
remind us of the constant need for growth and change. Our dogs will
always bring us the messages we need to hear regarding our issues
with loyalty and the coyotes will never stop howling at the moon,
reminding us about self-sabotage and to lighten up and not take ourselves so seriously. The butterfly that just climbed out of her cocoon
after transforming herself from a crawling caterpillar into a winged
wonder will flitter by just as we need to remember that we can also
change our lives and evolve into greater freedom and opportunity if
we take the time and find the courage to enter our introspective
cocoon to find the answers within. When we're stressed and anxious
the ants are right there at our feet to show us the power of patience
and perseverance. The owls will hoot to suggest we listen to the messages our Shadows are trying to send us in our dreams while we sleep,
and the hawks will screech to all who will listen, tuning us in again
and again to the need for expansive awareness. I believe Christ was
born in a barn for a reason—in the company of nature we are
immersed in the truth. Horses don't lie and neither do any of the animals in God's great kingdom. The magic is everywhere and serendip-
itous messages from the One are all around us and available all the
time. Thank God we have the horses to teach us how to listen.

[ACKNOWLEDGMENTS]

THANKS ARE DUE first and foremost to my best friend and muse, my wife Kathryn. I could not keep the pace over the long run without her outstanding support, inspiration, and willingness to ride the waves of change with me. Thanks also to my oldest friend and writing partner Bob Weber for his wisdom and talent. My hat is off to Matthew Lore, my publisher, for believing in my message and giving me a free rein to express myself. I also bow to my students, the many men and women who have the integrity and open-mindedness to learn how to play horse games, by horse rules, in order to be the best that they can be. And last but not least, I especially thank the horses. To err is human, to forgive is equine, and I most humbly thank all the horses, especially Stella, for so patiently showing me the way back to my heart.